HOW TO RUN FOR PUBLIC OFFICE, AND WIN!

by

Hugh Scott

Joseph S Reinicho

THE NATIONAL PRESS INC.

128 C STREET, N.E.

WASHINGTON, D. C. 20002

To

ALICE AND NORMAN

And Their Hostages To Fortune

Contents

PREFACE

SOME eighteen years ago, I spoke of the hundreds of young men and women who had expressed to me their dissatisfaction with the world of political things as they are, with the shortcomings of government and the shortfalls of political parties.

So I wrote a book about how to become a part of the political system aimed at those who might be persuaded to enter by that gate to work in the political vineyard. For reasons many and varied, thousands of them have done so. Whether the new grapes have bettered the taste of the wine is a matter of opinion. I, for one, favor the somewhat more sophisticated bouquet of these more recent vintages.

At the very time of that essay in political exposition, circumstances were engulfing me in a struggle for personal survival in political life, time, energy and spirit. I was able, nevertheless, to note that "this book would not leave me alone until I had written it."

The late Senator Dick Neuberger loved to accuse me, in light raillery, of having incited him to run for the Senate. The eminent John Minor Wisdom of New Orleans (now a U.S. Circuit Judge in the Circuit Court of Appeals for the Fifth District) tells me that he read the book preliminary to entering a sharp political fray ending in the overthrow of his party's leadership—and his succession to that leadership—in Louisiana.

On the other hand, candor compels the admission that another who told me he decided to enter politics after reading my book was twice defeated for Governor of Iowa.

These past two decades have seen notable improvements in the rapidity and effectiveness with which we communicate with one another. The intricate web of television networks and stations which reach even the most remote areas, the advent of color television, the still expanding communications satellite systems, the pending plans for a public television network, the presence of radios and TV's in cars, bedrooms, bathrooms and beside swimming pools, all these have generated new means and new habits in receiving information.

To these new indicia of an affluent society must be added the burgeoning of sophisticated public relations organizations, large and small, steadily tinkering with new political techniques.

I have often scoffed at the candidate who announces, with ruffles and flourishes, that he has been persuaded to offer himself on the altar of public service "at the request of thousands of my friends." I am wont to comment with that acerbity which has given me the local nickname of "the affable tiger" that the candidate's announcement boils down to the fact that he decided to run after talking it over with his wife.

It must be with some temerity then that I proffer a new book with the explanation that I have indeed been asked, on a respectable number of occasions, to write again on how to swim in political waters. Suggestions have come from public officials, potential candidates, teachers, but in the greatest number from college students, especially those interested in political youth organizations or in college intern programs in Washington. Without doubt the most important suggestion came (like the candidate consulting his wife) after talking it over with Jim Clay, my publisher.

This book, consonant with the changing times, offers not only new material but also a change of emphasis. While adhering to advice as to the ways of political life, I have added more discussion of the actual conduct of political campaigns and the role of the new breed of public relations specialists.

I hope that not only he who runs may read but that he who reads may run—for public office.

Imprimis, the earlier book would not let me alone.

In finis, I could not let this later effort alone until I had committed it.

I do hope that you will enjoy reading about politics as much as I relish working at it.

*   *   *

I renew my thanks to those who helped me with the original "how to" book. I am grateful also to Robert L. Kunzig, Eugene Cowen and George L. Stark, who taught me so much of the art of political persuasion during my campaigns. I add my thanks to The National Press Inc. for their interest in this new venture, and especially to James Clay and Stephen Horn for their encouragement.

My thanks also to my wife, who still patiently puts up with a man with his head in too many books. My especial bow to her for suggesting the book's original title. My gratitude is warmly extended to those who helped me get to galleys with this fifth undertaking, as with some of the others: Miss Edith V. Skinner, Miss Margaret Lynch, Mrs. Charles Arnold, Mr. Richard Murphy, Mr. Barton Hertzbach and Mr. Martin Hamberger.

HUGH SCOTT
U.S. Senator

1. Politics — and You

THEIR Royal Highnesses, the Duke and the Duchess of Kent were there.

The occasion: the world premiere, in Hell's own colors, of the tragedy of "Dr. Faustus" at the Queen's Theatre, Oxford. Later, at the supper for the starring Richard Burton and Elizabeth Taylor, I sat amidst my own world whose players are also always "on stage": politicians. This time, Members of Parliament, Labor and Conservative.

To the Lord President of the Council, a leader of Her Majesty's Government, I ventured: "Do you believe that the democracies, like Dr. Faustus, are selling their souls to the Devil in exchange for the new knowledge we have gained in technology and warmaking?"

"Oh, I should think not," was his answer, "but we'd best watch it."

How to go about watching it, how to watch it more diligently, is what I'm going to talk about in these chapters.

This was written in the halls of Oxford, one of the world's oldest universities, where I was lecturing on "the U.S. Political System" at Balliol College. Balliol, incidentally, has produced more men prominent in the government of Great Britain than perhaps any other institution within the past century. It has been turning out politicians, for that matter, for more than seven hundred years.

My legislative life in Washington involves continuing contacts with visiting students at high school, college and university level. I have addressed students at scores of colleges, taking part in their rallies, contended at their mock conventions. In all of

1

my eleven political campaigns, young workers have been zealous and tireless in carrying the standard of their candidates to every corner of the constituency. Their enthusiasm is beyond price, their efforts truly tireless.

Every summer, about a dozen young collegians, men and women, work in my office, meet my constituents and breathe the sometimes heady air of political life.

They are, for the most part, idealistic. They are questing folk. How do you campaign? How do you handle people? How do you follow legislation through? How do you make up your mind? How closely do you listen and take advice from your constituents?

One question is overriding. It was, as I fully expected, the first question posed after my first lecture for Balliol in the draughty old Examination Schools' high-ceilinged hall: "How do I get into politics?"

Politics and I are old hat. Politics and you is the subject which interests me most of all. For you are the replacements for the troops.

Is youth in revolt? Enough, I think, to be healthy, but no more, I surmise, than many of their predecessors. Certainly youth today is no more, and hopefully no less, aware of what can go wrong among free but careless people than was the young Thomas Jefferson when he laid it down that "it is fitting that the tree of liberty be watered from time to time by the blood of tyrants," nor when he reminded us that the ultimate sovereign right of any people is the right of revolution. Who uses any stronger words today?

Youth and dissent are synonymous. This must be so, if they are to march, armed with their convictions, in the ranks of those who rebel against ignorance.

Some know, with Goethe, that "nothing is more terrible than ignorance in action."

All youth are aware that wars are the end product of bad diplomacy and that it is the young who must fight the wars the old have made.

Are not the protest movements simply saying: there has to be a better way?

Well, doesn't there?

If so, who will find it? Who will challenge with informed action the cynical old definition of a democracy as "government of the indifferent by the ignorant for the benefit of the incompetent"?

You.

You, or those like you, one fervently hopes.

Whether it will be for the greater glory of the republic only time can tell. To those who fear that the soul of the democracies is already in pawn for Satan's apple of unlocked knowledge, I can only affirm, being of no little faith in man and man's future.

I am no pessimist.

Read on!

2. How to Get Started

Is it hard to get into politics?

How do you go about it?

Are there special rules to follow?

Can I get started on my own or whom do I go to see?

How you start depends a good deal on where you start. If you live in a small town or in the country, your beginnings will differ somewhat from an entry into city politics. And geography has a good deal to do with it too. Obviously, conditions vary considerably between the Middle West and the South, for example, and activity in a two-party community differs from politics where a single party is dominant or where little attention is paid to party labels in local affairs.

The last fifteen years have brought great changes to the U.S. political map, perhaps the most significant reshuffling of allegiances in a hundred years. There are far fewer one-party states. Smaller one-party political units are also moving toward either a two-party system or nonpartisan election of local officials.

The impact of historic Supreme Court decisions in decreeing compulsory reapportionment of State legislative and U.S. Congressional districts in accordance with its "one man, one vote" doctrine has drastically accelerated a trend, already well underway, toward more competitive election contests. Shifting populations and changing allegiances have contributed to the emergence of fairly evenly divided two-party states where only one party had long flourished. While the number of marginal Congressional seats is little more than one-fourth of the House of Representatives, few Senate seats and hardly any governorships can now be regarded as safely in the grasp of a single political party.

Two-party politics is now the order of the day in once rockbound Republican Maine, New Hampshire, Iowa, South Dakota and Kansas, as Democratic Governors or Senators or both exemplify. In the once "Solid South," no longer can the Democratic Party take elections for granted. Florida, Arkansas and Oklahoma have elected Republican Governors and Republicans sit in the Senate from the old Confederate bastions of South Carolina and Texas, not to speak of the border states where the phenomenon is a little less surprising. Southern Republican seats in the House have multiplied to 23, more than fourfold in a brief decade.

As the two-party system spreads into the electoral nooks and crannies and "safe" seats move into the doubtful column at all political levels, all sorts of new opportunities are opening up to attract new and venturesome political talent.

This flooding of the hitherto stagnant one-party ponds should tempt new would-be swimmers to try the water.

Before testing the temperature with a tentative toe, it might be well to cast up accounts with yourself before you get too far from shore.

Why do you want to get into politics at all?

If you intend to make a career of political activity, don't hesitate to admit to yourself your self-interest, your hope for some advantage to yourself. But it is a good guess that if self-interest is your only motive, you're going to make no more than a fair-to-middling politician at best. The rule of politics is the same as the rule of life in general: you get out about what you put in. I have no wish to belabor you with the overworked phrase "public service," but it is solid fact, which any good politician will verify, that you will find politics a great deal more satisfying if you enter it with a genuine desire to be

5

helpful to other people and to use your widening influence for local, state, or national betterment.

Right here I readily grant that there are a lot of politicians who don't, whose only goal is what may be in it for them, what they personally will get out of it. But in comparison with the few unlovely characters who have risen to power and held it with callous indifference to anything but their own aggrandizement, consider the many who, having no higher standard than their own advantage, have found this to be a self-limiting horizon as they plod morosely through minor jobs, holding the respect of no one and with little or no hope of advancement.

Furthermore, I am assuming that you are not that sort of person. If you are, there is plenty of room for you in politics— at the bottom. Since you aren't, then I suggest that you work out in your own mind the kind of political career you think will offer the most real compensation in terms of enjoyment of the work you would like to do, of opportunity to see things done better under your guiding hand, of the solid satisfaction that comes from community appreciation of services which are recognized as in the public's interest.

Having decided then that you would like to aim for a career as a public prosecutor or tax specialist, a city planner or agricultural-laboratory experimentalist, or that your yen runs toward elective office as city councilman, state or national legislator, what do you do next? Nothing is more certain than that, in politics, you do not simply file an application at the front office. You know, that really does happen sometimes. It happens just about as often as a small-town blonde lands in Hollywood stardom after a cold canvass of the situation and an application for the job. But the spectacle of a political unknown bursting suddenly on the elective or appointive scene, without prior political activity or experience, happens just often enough to encourage political counterparts of the Hollywood hopefuls to file, unsupported, for elective office, or to besiege appointive authorities with letters and visits with exhaustive (and exhausting) accounts of their qualifications.

All of which is by way of leading up to what is probably fairly obvious to you anyway, namely, that the best way to begin in politics is at the beginning. So, how does one go about it?

The whole political show may appear to you to be the veriest maze with no beginning or ending to it, the actors moving about on sundry levels. The tyro wonders how they got there and whether the whole thing is done with mirrors. There *is* a definite pattern, which is subject to dissection and analysis. The maze has its entrances and its exits.

Although the terminology will vary between rural and urban areas or in various sections of the country, the basic organization of a political party is much the same wherever found. I am going to choose for illustration, because it is the species of party organization with which I am most familiar, the manner in which a major party operates in a large city.

Cities are divided into wards or aldermanic districts, some of which may be much larger in population or area than others. Owing to failure to reapportion or inequities in reapportionment, there are still some "rotten boroughs" among these civic subdivisions, and therefore political power may often be exercised by some leaders out of all proportion to the area or population represented by them in relation to the whole city.

The wards or aldermanic districts are in turn divided into precincts or divisions. There may be anywhere from one division to a hundred divisions in a ward. The size of a division may be two or three city blocks, or it may be a square mile or much greater in the more sparsely settled suburban areas (of course these subdivisions are still larger in rural areas). The voting population of a division may run from two or three hundred voters to a thousand, or even fifteen hundred. Rotten boroughs again. An average division will contain about six or seven hundred voters.

Again for purposes of illustration, let us suppose that the city has fifty wards and that a given ward has forty divisions. In each of these divisions each political party will usually have two local residents serving as division committeemen (or women) or precinct captains, as they are sometimes called. They are elected for a term of years by the members of their respective parties living and voting in the division. Vacancies in these posts are usually filled in the interim between elections by selection of a substitute at a meeting of the ward or aldermanic district committee.

Since each division has two committeemen and our specimen ward has forty divisions, there will be eighty committeemen to comprise the ward (or aldermanic district) committee. Following their election, at a meeting of the ward committee called for the purpose these committeemen elect a ward representative to the party's city committee, sometimes called the city campaign committee or city party organization. This representative is commonly referred to as the ward leader, ward committeeman, or district leader.

Since we are assuming a city of fifty wards, there will be fifty representatives to the party's central city committee. These representatives, or ward leaders, in turn elect a city chairman of their political party, who becomes known in common parlance as a leader of the Republican or Democratic organization and is unfailingly referred to in opposition newspapers as the Republican or Democratic boss. It may be added that, in political repartee, one's own party is usually the Party while the opposition is ordinarily dismissed as the Machine or the Gang. I seem to recall from my schoolboy Latin studies that Cicero used the same verbal witchcraft.

The city chairman, or party leader, supervises the multifarious activities at political headquarters in the interim between primary elections (or conventions in some states) and general elections. While Joe Doakes slumbers except on election day—and often then, too—the practicing politician knows that politics is a 365-day-a-year job and that elections are usually won or lost long before the polls open. Knowing this, the city chairman's time is taken up daily with visits from ward leaders looking for jobs for the faithful in their wards, or seeking municipal improvements in their areas, such as new sewers, roads, or street lights. Here is an interesting fact not often noted in the public prints: in most communities, far more improvements in civic or rural living are obtained from the cities, counties, or states through this kind of intercession (which springs from pragmatic reasons of political advantage) than results from the far better publicized campaigns of taxpayers' leagues, reform organizations, or newspaper crusades. For this, score a point on the plus side for the much maligned "Organization."

It should be noted here that the massive intervention of the Federal government in such areas as housing, relief of poverty and education has, to a degree, minimized the influence of the political leaders. Federal administrative appointments for reasons of patronage is quite common.

The city chairman is also likely to spend much time in ironing out differences within the city organization, that is, among the ward leaders. Humanly enough, almost any ward leader is chronically beset with the conviction that far more jobs and improvements are going to other wards than his own; the city chairman needs all the tact at his command to handle these situations. If too many ward leaders become dissatisfied, there may be a new city chairman next time.

The day of the ton of coal in the voter's cellar and the Christmas basket on his table is pretty well past, as the state and federal governments have been persuaded that relief of the less fortunate is the duty of all the people. The donors still seek to retain the political gratitude of the donees by reminders at election time of the claimed source of the benefactions. But the sound political maxim that you had better be at the voter's side when he needs you if you want him to be at your side when you need him will probably never cease to be a truism. So the problems of the individual voter, as well as the local community needs for new paved streets, parks, playgrounds, and swimming pools, are often in the mind of the ward leader.

As election time approaches, the city chairman's working day grows longer. New personnel are added at headquarters; various campaign subcommittees are set up; a speaker's bureau goes into action; the public relations men and women swing into high gear; statements, news releases, and predictions come in from the printer and pour out to the press and to the ward leaders, committeemen, and volunteer workers; advertisements, campaign posters, and circulars are prepared, television and radio time obtained and allotted; and a sizable increase of adrenalin is noted in the political circulatory system. All this costs money and a finance committee goes out to fill the war chest, supplied with lists of prospects to be turned over to a corps of fund solicitors who pass the word that "now is the time to come to the aid of the party." So much, for the time being, for the staff work.

Similar to the Army, all is built around the infantry as the only tactical unit which can take and hold the ground gained, so in any political organization the division committeeman, the private soldier of politics, is the indispensable basic unit upon whom success depends. The saying is often heard in politics: "This is a committeeman's fight." Its usual connotation is that the particular election under discussion depends for its outcome, not on issues or personalities of the candidates, but on the zeal and effectiveness of the party workers in getting out the vote. Actually every election is a committeeman's fight. This the good committeeman knows full well, and the more acutely aware of it the ward leader or city chairman is, the better the results are likely to be.

The competent committeeman knows that the success of his tactics at the polls depends upon the strategy he has followed the rest of the year. If he has earned the good will of his neighbors through making himself well known to them and helping them when they need help, he will be that much more likely to persuade them to support the candidates of his party at the polls on election day. If he has not bothered to become acquainted with the people in his division or has failed to consult, advise and help them, they in turn may listen to the committeeman of the opposing party whose record with them has been better, or they may simply ignore him as an anonymous nuisance, trying to thrust a sample ballot into their hands at the polling place. Or not having been *invited* to vote, they may stay away from the polls altogether. Perhaps you wonder at the reference to being invited to exercise their right to vote. I am sure you would be amazed at the number of people who have become so used to having their franchise solicited at election time that, upon default of a visit from their committeeman, they will sit home on election day in high dudgeon, their feelings woefully hurt, because they have not been urged, *i.e.,* invited, to perform their civic duty!

Not the least of the committeeman's duties is to see that the voter is qualified to vote by compliance with the local registration and absentee voting laws. In fact, this is his most important responsibility. Obviously, a voter who isn't registered can't vote. And since potential voters are notoriously negligent about this, many votes will be lost unless the citizen is jogged and reminded by someone, which means the committeeman, that he has not yet registered and is informed of the time and place where he can qualify himself to vote. Again, if he knows and likes the committeeman, and especially if he has been the recipient of some service from the latter, he or she is more likely to leave the office or the shopping tour or the household duties a little early in order to register. Commentary: ask any committeeman how

11

often the loudest griper about political conditions turns out to be unregistered!

Now that we have had a quick look at the hierarchy of a political party and have seen that it all comes down to the committeeman, we are back at the beginning. This is where we came in. Or, perhaps, this is where you come in. I once asked the head of the Carnegie Foundation how I might qualify for a scholarship, one of a number to be awarded by them. He told me this story. One day a stranger approached Aesop and inquired how long it would take him to reach Athens. Aesop said, "I don't know." The stranger started off down the highway, and when he had gone a few yards, Aesop called to him and said, "It will take you two hours." The stranger turned angrily, "You are a stupid yokel; why didn't you tell me that before?" And Aesop said only, "How could I tell how long it would take you until I saw how fast you walked?"

If you are going into politics, if you decide to make the journey to some political Athens, no one else can tell you how long it will be before you come into sight of your appointed goal until he has had a chance to form a judgment of your capacity, until he sees how fast you walk. But one thing is fairly certain; unless you are unusually favored by circumstance, you will begin the journey on foot. There are the usual exceptions that prove the rule; wealthy campaign contributors have begun as ambassadors (to the disgust of the career men in the State Department) and the son or even the brother of a governor or president may skip some of the steps up the ladder. But these unearned increments are a phenomenon in the business world, too, and about as infrequent.

I have gone into some detail about the duties of the privates, the company commanders, field and staff officers of a political army, chiefly in order to emphasize the importance of the services of the division committeeman. I wish to make it clear that normally one's chances of further political preferment are greatly enhanced by willingness to serve in the ranks, to contribute to the success of one's party in order to share in political preferment.

It is not in my mind to give the impression that one who thus enters politics does so with a view of advancement to ward leadership or to chairmanship of a political party unit. The contrary is usually so. There are some who have this ambition and who progress through a lifetime from one professional political post to another, and who usually receive recognition by election or appointment to public office, roughly equivalent in status to the value and importance of their political leadership.

There are many others, including business and professional men, labor union officials or workers who enter politics without any thought of advancing in the political hierarchy as such. Some of them enjoy participation in politics for the love of it, some because the contacts are thought to be helpful in their organization or profession, and sometimes recognition arrives without planning for it. I think it will be agreed by most observers of the political scene that most committeemen and committeewomen have their eye on obtaining some appointive or elective office—if not for themselves, then for some member of their family—which they hope to merit through favorable reaction to their work in their neighborhoods. There is often active competition for appointment and advancement, most noticeable on election night when successful committeemen announce the returns from their division with pride, amid a certain amount of fanfare and excitement.

There is a *quid pro quo* involved: the worker advances the fortunes of the party; in doing so, he counts on recognition of the value of his contribution. As the Italian proverb has it, "Una mano lava l'altra e tutte due lavano il viso." ("One hand washes the other and both hands wash the face.")

Is this peculiar to politics?

3. Making the Grade

MAKING a start in politics as a committeeman isn't the only way. You could begin by service on the speaker's bureau in a political campaign, for example. If you do, a national campaign involving a presidential election offers the best opportunity, because the need for and receptivity to volunteers is at the peak. At times it seems that everyone who ever had the remotest interest in politics is active in some direction in a presidential campaign; many of them are never heard from again, or at least not for another four years. But if you have ability as a speaker, as a solicitor of campaign funds, or as an administrator or organizer, here is an opportunity for you to get in the swim where the water is warm and inviting.

Go to the chairman of the political committee or to the chairman of the speaker's bureau or finance committee, tell him what you think you can do, get an assignment, and show all and sundry that you can do it. Don't wait too long to apply; there are usually more offers to help than can be handled. Go in the early organizational stages and if you are given the brush-off, try again. Return with reinforcements, such as a phone call or letter of recommendation from someone well known to the chairman. Be prepared to be given routine or pedestrian assignments at first. Count on doing an outstanding job as the best route to more interesting work and a greater share in political activity. If your offer to help in the campaign is accepted and you are thereafter given no work to do, something is wrong somewhere. Go to the chairman and tell him so; if this doesn't work, go to the general chairman in that community. If you have ability, he will be glad to use it; that's why he was put there, to get the best results out of the most people. But don't expect miracles. Expect to be told that you can do your best work on your own street, among your neighbors. You won't be *Mr. Smith Goes to Washington* in your first role. That's just Hollywood again.

Then again, you can enter politics as an independent. Under our two-party system, very little is heard in national campaigns of independents who are without some affiliation with one of the two major parties, although third parties do spring up from time to time and shortly disappear. People are sometimes called independents who should more properly be designated as Democrats supporting a Republican candidate or vice versa. Some communities have or have had active independent voters' organizations, such as the Charter party in Cincinnati or the City party of 1905 in Philadelphia. In some cities, such as Detroit or Los Angeles, local elections for municipal office are, at least technically, on a nonpartisan basis, in that candidates who may be registered Democrats or Republicans do not run for office under such designations in municipal elections. In many smaller communities national party designations have little or no significance in local elections. And this is especially true in one-party areas, as in some Southern enclaves.

You will find that, where independent voters' organizations exist in addition to the regular party organizations, if you so desire you will usually be welcomed into membership as an independent. Your rise to recognition may seem to be somewhat more rapid than in the more rigidly constituted party organizations. Also, if you have aggressiveness and color, you may find yourself in a fairly short time an independent candidate for some elective office. All of this may look like the royal road to political eminence, which I have elsewhere indicated didn't exist, but there is a catch to it. In spite of the apparent merit in some of the programs advocated by independent groups, you aren't likely to be on the winning side in many elections. Independent

15

movements usually fail through lack of continuity, grass roots organization, and political know-how. Their occasional successes over the major political parties occur at moments of intense public reaction against one or both of the latter. If the independent group's program has captured the public's imagination or promises to furnish a vehicle (sometimes in "fusion" with one of the major parties) to punish the party in power, it may win success at the polls. These so-called reform movements generally have a one-term life span as the public sighs and concludes (not necessarily correctly) that in putting them into office, it mistook zeal for efficiency.

So your city or town or county returns to its political faith, settles down to being Democratic or Republican again and the leaders of the two parties look askance at you and wonder if you really believed all the things you perspired for or whether you were just trying to make a name for yourself. In any event, the party organizations are likely to be wary of you and your company, for the present, unless you have demonstrated such political appeal as to attract a personal following or such perspicacity as to make you a desirable acquisition. In that case the political portals of the Elephant or the Donkey will yawn for you. You will be made to feel that bygones are bygones, only we hope you won't do such a foolish thing again!

No, starting as a committeeman or precinct captain isn't the only way. All things considered, it is probably the best way. If you are zealous to improve political conditions where you live, you will be in a better position to do it if you have learned something about politics from the inside and from the ground up. If you have proved yourself to be a good hard-working committeeman, you have already improved matters to that extent; perhaps you will be inspired to take a more active interest, widening the scope of your influence as time goes on.

As I have said, division committeemen are usually elected by the voters of the same political party resident in the division.

In those localities where this is not the case, selection may be made by a party committee or convention. In any event, the technique of getting started is the same. There may already be a vacancy in your division; inquiry in the neighborhood or at the local political headquarters or club will soon get you this information. If there is, and you want to be considered for the vacancy, go directly to the leader of your ward (or comparable political unit) and tell him so. Tell him something about yourself and why you want to get into politics. He is rather likely to welcome your offer and to undertake to propose your name for the vacant place. The very fact that there is a vacancy is some indication that the ward leader may have been looking around for someone competent to fill it. On the other hand, the politico may not want to fill it if he is, for example, of the minority party and may have an understanding with the majority party organization locally to keep the party turnout at elections low in number in exchange for such favors as building permits, zoning variances, liquor licenses—not to mention tickets to the ball game. Or the political leader, if of the majority party, may feel that he is getting an adequate voting turnout without encouraging the kind of new worker who might offer political competition to him. With a little diligence, you can always root out the true situation, and if the office is elective, you can file for it and force the hand of the political establishment.

Perhaps you will find that in your neighborhood both committeemen are very much on the job and have no present intention of resigning or moving away. In that case don't decide to retire from politics for the present. The turnover in committeemen is always considerable; meanwhile, there is work you can be doing. Talk to the leader of the ward anyway, and ask him to introduce you to the present committeemen or committeewomen. Tell them you want to help them in the division and ask them to let you work with them in getting out the vote on election day or in working at the polls. Some committeemen are jealous of their prerogatives and will discourage this. If this happens, you can still do volunteer work at the polls on your own, thus getting acquainted with the voters; or you can take to the sidelines, meanwhile improving your acquaintance in the neighborhood, and wait for a vacancy or for the election of new committeemen, at which time you can file for the nomination. This is a simple procedure, in most states requiring only the signature of a few of your neighbors on a petition. Then you can square off to fight it out with the incumbents. This will give you valuable experience—and helpful bumps perhaps—and if you are willing to talk personally with enough of your neighbors, you have a good chance to win the first time around. If both the present committeemen are well known and popular, you may not make it on your first try, but you have already made yourself known to a number of people who will provide a nucleus for your next effort. Actually, one of the present committeemen is likely to be superior to the other and you may nose out the less popular or less efficient one.

Most committeemen will welcome rather than discourage your offer to help. They will need helpers at the polls, watchers (who are designated to protect the interest of candidates or parties) and election officials, such as judges and inspectors of election. They may also need clerks or baby sitters or car drivers to assist in the registration of voters.

There is no better way to gain practical political experience than by the mutual help and exchange of views which will come from membership in the local group of Young Republicans or Young Democrats, or independent or nonpartisan study groups, according to your political leanings. I commend these organizations to you. They will be glad to have you and you will gain from your association with them. And if there is no such outfit in your community, you will gain even more experience—and recognition—by joining with like-minded persons in getting such a group under way. A sample constitution and by-laws may be found at the end of this book as Appendix A.

It is vital to the usefulness as well as to the internal health of these party youth organizations that their ranks be steadily replenished by young Americans with the will to learn, apply and fairly use the political experience to be gained in group activity.

There is danger to the effective working of the political system when youth auxiliaries, because of the apathy or indifference of the general membership, fall into the hands of a small group of zealously self-perpetuating extremists. With increased membership and, importantly, increasingly alert members, there is a better chance for leaders and membership to draw closer— and more realistically—to the views of the rank and file of the party in general. To lapse into aphorism again, furious activity cannot always be equated with constructive action.

An excellent way for a tyro to test out his interest in politics is to join one of the business-oriented or civic or labor union political action groups. The technique of non-party (though sometimes party-affiliated) units designed to elect candidates or influence legislation was first perfected by the CIO (Council of Industrial Organizations) soon after its emergence as a powerful factor in labor relations. The practice soon caught on in the American Federation of Labor. To avoid the restrictions in Federal labor-management legislation against direct participation by labor unions or corporations in political campaigns, the presently merged AFL-CIO has established national and local "political education" bodies. The right of these associations to engage in political action, including the vital power to raise money through so-called voluntary dues assessments, has been sustained by the courts. For those members objecting to the 'check-off' or imposition of a part of their wages to support a party not of their choice, the courts have tended to permit reimbursement or have insisted that 'voluntary' cannot include involuntary deductions.

Somewhat belatedly, corporations, beginning with some of the larger corporate units and gradually proliferating, have established their own political action groups. Their techniques in flattering imitation of union initiative include voluntary attendance at sessions for instruction in politics, including addresses by public officials at various levels and exhortations to engage as workers or candidates in political campaigns.

Some civic organizations engage in similar activities, including chambers of commerce, trade associations, farm organizations, the League of Women Voters and a number of pressure groups often sponsoring legislation which they believe to be in their interest.

Joining any group to which you are eligible is easy. Rising to leadership involves, of course, application to the affairs of the group, the commitment of a certain amount of time in attendance and service and, certainly, the ability to attract favorable consideration.

So you begin your apprenticeship in the great art of politics, and, in time, you will either grow bored with the whole thing, or it will get into your blood and you're hooked. You are likely to be politicking all your life. If you stick at the apprenticeship for a while, you may well bob up as the logical candidate for the first vacancy on the ward committee.

As the committeeman, your principal job will be to know as much as possible about the voting habits of the people in your division, which ones can be counted on to come out and vote without urging, which ones have to be invited, which are politically unreliable (some politicians call them cheaters), which ones must have transportation to the polls, which voters in the other party may possibly be converted or at least proselytized to vote for some of your candidates, and which ones are indebted to the party as job holders or to a committeeman for some service previously rendered. This fund of information is usually acquired by a more or less frequent canvass of the division.

Pleasant relations, on a basis of friendly rivalry, are generally maintained with the committeemen of the opposite political party. Over the years, many of my good friends have sat on the opposite side of the political aisle. Information is often obtained that way as to who has moved in or out of the division, for example. Also, pleasant relations are better than unpleasant relations on general principle. The rivalry for votes at the general election will be none the less keen because of it.

In the interim between elections the help or advice of the committeeman is often solicited by his neighbors. The families in a certain street complain of the potholes in the highway, or they think it is time they got the promised sewer system, or more street lighting is needed, or more police protection against violence or delinquency. The committeeman is told all about it. Generally speaking, the poorer the conditions, the more work for the committeeman. He is also asked to help someone get on the police force or to see that Mrs. Robinson's husband is put under a peace bond by the magistrate or justice of the peace so he won't keep scaring Mrs. Robinson out of her wits every time he comes home charged with that poison again. From assessments to zoo picnics, the committeeman hears all about it.

He attends, with his colleagues on the committee, the meetings of the ward committee. The principal subjects under discussion there are ways and means of getting the maximum number of voters registered and what is to be done to achieve success in the next election.

The committeeman also manages to become well known in the community by attending all neighborhood meetings, socials, picnics, clambakes, rallies, sports, and any other occasion where the gregarious have agglomerated. There he circulates, to good advantage, a sympathetic ear cocked, a friendly hand extended, to one and all. All of these doings come under the head of inculcating good will.

It is at the polls that the committeeman really comes under the guns; it is up to him to make the best possible showing. The more people who know him and, better still, the more people who like him, the better his chances of getting them to come out to the polls and, once there, to vote for the candidates for whom the committeeman is plugging.

Do I hear you saying that this is far from an ideal situation, that the sovereign voter should cast his vote solely on the merits of the issues and the candidates? I answer that of course he should, but where will he get this information? Newspapers of opposite political faith tell him yes and tell him no; speakers on the radio and television do the same thing; the billboards shriek contradictions at each other. I am writing of what is, rather than of what ought to be, and the fact is that the voter, countless thousands of him, when he sees a familiar and friendly face outside the polls, says, "Ah, here's my friend, Mr. Precinct. He will tell me who he thinks I should vote for." There are, at the same time, many other voters who have made up their minds as to the party and the candidate they prefer long before they go to the polls, and who march purposefully past the election workers and cast their ballots without more ado.

The committeeman is at the polls to corral all the votes he can. The competition that began with the candidates and continues in the newspapers, the radio, the TV, the billboards, the sound trucks, and the circulars carries on at the site of the ultimate decision, the polling place. The committeemen of the opposing political party are there to corral all the votes they can, too.

The committeeman is also at the polls to see that no bad apples get into the barrel. It is his job to see that people who are not registered do not vote and that no illegal votes are cast. Human nature being what it is, he is more apt to be on the lookout to challenge and to question the electoral qualifications of would-be voters of the opposite political faith. His opposite number in the other party is doing the same thing. The duly-appointed watchers have, in most states, this same right to challenge the voter's registration or other qualifications as an elector.

It behooves the committeeman or watcher or volunteer helper at the polls to familiarize himself or herself with the provisions of the registration and election laws.

This information is generally easily obtainable from the central committee of the party or from the party's legal counsel. It is often available in pamphlet form, containing relevant information as to length of residence required in state, county, and division, when and how registration and party affiliation may be changed, whether any other voting requirements exist, who may work in the polling place, how to challenge voters, and much other information of value to election workers.

The competent committeeman gets to know the voting habits of many of his neighbors. If Mr. Jones usually votes in the morning before going to work, his nonappearance is a signal to start looking around for him this year, but if he customarily votes when he comes home from work, there is no need to check up on him until an hour or so before the polls close. Knowing that the biggest voting rush comes after working hours as a rule and to avoid a jam at the polls in the closing hours, many committeemen and women make special efforts to get the housewives and the unemployed voters out during the middle hours of the day. For, so lightly is the franchise held by many, rather than queue up to vote, this type will go home without voting if the polling place is crowded.

Being a committeeman is not an end in itself if one may judge from the comments overheard from many of these hard workers in the political vineyard. It is rather a means to an end: a political job, candidacy, or the improvement of one's business or professional contacts. So, let us suppose you are now a committeeman, doing a good job at it and wondering what else you ought to be doing to advance your ambition to get somewhere in politics.

Since you are a good committeeman, you are already pretty well known in your own vicinity. How to become better known in your city or county? How to improve your prospects for political advancement? The Lord, it has been said so often, helps those who help themselves. You have made a good start at helping yourself by helping others in pursuing your duties as a division jack-of-all troubles. I would suggest that you go on from there, taking an ever-increasing part in community activities, help the Red Cross campaign, join a church, the young men's or young women's religious associations, the local businessmen's or farmer's association, as the case may be, tie in with those lodges or service clubs where you find congenial associations. The Young Republicans and Young Democrats offer invaluable political experience, and they will welcome your interest and your help. So will any of the other groups I have mentioned.

Don't be content with merely joining. Go on from there. I recently heard a minister give a talk, the theme of which was, "Are you a thermometer or a thermostat?" A thermometer, he said, just passively registers what's going on around it, whereas a thermostat does something about it. If you are going to be thermometer minded, save yourself the dues; don't bother to join all the organizations around. But if you would like to be of benefit to the community and benefit yourself at the same time, take an active part in these doings, share in the work and in the deliberations. People will get to know you, and you will learn who are the active doers and who are the drones among your acquaintances.

If you have a flair for public speaking, use it without overdoing it; moderation in all things is ever a good guide. If you would like to be a better public speaker, there are always instructors not too far away; good public speaking is mostly a matter of practice and growing self-confidence anyway. To gain that self-confidence you might join one of the Toastmaster Clubs to be found in most communities. They are banded together in a national organization. This way, you will kill two birds with one stone: improve your speaking ability at the same time you're meeting more people.

The ability to speak well in public (and not too long!) is an undoubted political asset. Lawyers may seem to have some advantage here since it is part of their professional day-to-day work, but the advantage is more apparent than real. The greatest asset of the good public speaker is the sincerity of his thought when coupled with simple clarity of expression; I am aware that this does not account for the success of some rabble-rousing demagogues. But some people love demagoguery and insist on being played for suckers. There will always be demagogues because there will always be certain people who will walk miles in the rain to hear them. Whatever your style of public speaking, try to avoid demogoguery like the plague. It is the height of indecency, political and otherwise, relying for its success upon appeals to chauvinism, xenophobia, bigotry, and intolerance. And don't hesitate to let people know that you hate it; that is a good way to win friends and influence decent people.

A word as to personality. This is no tract on how to be the life of the party, nor do I mean to suggest that it will help if you speak to the waiter in French, but a good personality is as much of an asset in politics as it is in business. It is important for you to like people and to be genuinely interested in them if you expect a reciprocal reaction. You will need tact and ever so much patience; you will need to think clearly and logically through to a reasoned conclusion. You will need courage, which will be often tested.

A good digestion, to survive numberless political banquets, will help too!

4. What Counts Most

THE main track of this chapter will deal with personality traits, the possession or acquisition of which are helpful to politically active men and women.

But before we leave the station let it be clearly understood that both background and training are not at all minimized. The experience of growing up in a household of politically alert relatives, or of early association with people who are civic minded, is quite obviously advantageous.

So likewise will it be most helpful to acquire as much of political science, civics, history, economics, logic, and social studies generally as one can manage during one's school life or as a part of one's voluntary outside reading.

It will be especially helpful to find temporary employment, paid or voluntary, in the office of a public official, preferably an elected one. This furnishes excellent on-the-job training. Relatively new on the political scene and offering first-rate opportunities for practical insight into the political world are the increasingly popular "college intern" programs. No longer fed by a few large universities but available now to students generally are summer jobs in the offices of legislators and in the executive departments of state and federal governments. Some go by selection, some by competition. Students, usually seniors, postgraduates or recent graduates apply to their own congressman or senator or to any executive agency. While some complain of routine duties, most offices provide an intermix of the ordinary daily round with an opportunity to attend committee or legislative sessions, research projects, legislation or speeches, sit in on conferences with constituents or guide visitors around the capital city.

Ten or twelve college interns serve in my office each summer and take turns at those duties which are respectively the more or the less interesting. They come from many different colleges and universities and manage to make an informative stay of it, not alone because of the nature of their duties but by virtue of the chance to hear talks by party leaders and others in both parties. They usually combine forces with other offices to set up entertainment programs and to publish their own 'house organ.' Some years the President addresses the assembled interns. The Vice President always does. I have been pressed into trying a hand at the drums during a summer visit by the Newport Jazz Festival. Confrontations among Senatorial softball teams are, if not legendary, strenuously contested.

Leland Stanford Jr. University founded a "Stanford-In-Washington" program in 1963 which has grown from 13 to 85 students. Wellesley established its program even earlier. There is a Pennsylvania college program managed from Franklin and Marshall College.

Among the more senior programs, the Ford Foundation has sponsored state internships in the California Legislature. Fellows of the American Political Science Association have brought young political scientists, lawyers and journalists to state capitals and to Washington where they work with experienced politicians of their choice. Some of these young men and women work and study for a year, serving for half that time with a legislator of one party and the remainder with a member of the other party.

Interns brighten the summer scene in Washington immeasurably and clog up the Capital's cafeterias considerably.

A number have stayed on as top assistants or valued researchers or speech writers. Quite a few have run for office. One young woman, finishing her internship in my office, discovered that the only remaining duty of the Coroner's office in Mercer County, New Jersey was to provide relief for shipwrecked seaman. To try her hand at campaigning, she ran for the office on a write-in ballot appeal and was elected. Princeton has no seacoast, so she has time to ponder more ambitious ventures.

I must add that I have never known a college intern from my office who has not retained, at the least as an informed observer, a lively interest in politics.

You will be wise to look around for the best tools for your chosen trade. "For upon wisdom is a house builded, and with knowledge shall its chambers be filled. . . ."

Speaking of personality, what quality of heart or mind can be regarded as being the most desirable in the political practitioner? Is there any one definable quality he will need more than any other, some one element in his make-up that must take clear primacy over all others? The answer to this is easy: The indispensable element for success in politics is integrity. And it is a quality of the heart first and of the mind second.

A man of moderate intellect and unquestioned integrity may go far, without stain upon his record; a brilliantly gifted charlatan will, soon or late, fall into public disrespect or degradation, his good name tarnished although his wealth in terms of money and goods may show no diminution. Does some public figure pop into your mind as an outstanding exception? If it does, he is. That means that others have noted this too, and the stain is there and the shadow on his name. Wait a while; the accounting is shaping up for him. It is not idly written that "a good name is more to be desired than great riches."

"An honest man's the noblest work of God"—and the best politician. Raymond Swing, the commentator, once said to me, "I think the average politician has a higher standard of honesty than the average businessman. This is no reflection on the businessman, but the politician has to be honest. It is the most valuable tool of his trade." And this is bound to be true if you will reflect on it. One's success in politics rests upon keeping one's promises to those who have asked that something or other be done for them.

Keeping one's word is the first commandment of politics. The word of the politician must be as good as his bond; for if it is not, the penalties are sure and relentless: others lose confidence in him, the intangible but very real asset of good will fades away, the support of his friends diminishes, and the political potency that once was his is lost. He may carry on for a while in the office he holds, but his days are numbered as the word goes around that "you can't rely on him." For this very reason, promises are not given too freely or readily by the wise politician. More often one hears, "I'll try," "I'll do the best I can," "I'll look into it and let you know," "I'll see what can be done." This is often exasperating to the citizen with a problem, and he is apt to be critical of this kind of treatment. But he has not put himself in the other fellow's place nor given thought to what his own later reaction will be if, after what he takes to be a firm promise, he is subsequently disappointed.

In the long run, "I'll try" is a lot more satisfactory than "I'll surely do it for you" unless you know you surely can, and in politics how can you know until you have tried?

Unlike some of the other traits of personality helpful to a politician, this capacity for being trusted, if not inborn, is not one that may be easily acquired by practice and determined application. Guile and slickness are not permanently concealed from the observant by mere adherence to the letter of one's agreement. Perhaps it may be possible to classify political trustworthiness into three groups: the man who can be trusted because he can be trusted, who is honorable because it is not in his make-up to be otherwise; the man who will be trusted because he has found that honesty pays and has exhibited it in his prior conduct; the man who cannot be trusted.

As I set these observations down, I am aware of the overtones of cynicism, of the occasional sour notes that creep in. Remember please, gentle would-be politico, that this is no ghostwritten political biography, contracted for to build up some public figure or to advance some ideology, left, center, or right; it is an effort to set down some thoughts on the methods of political man, some views on what politics is really like. And if it will not all come out white, it won't come out all black either. I hope you will come to agree with me that the total effect is rather more checkerboard than the dull indefiniteness of tattletale gray.

Well, after integrity, what? As I have said, I think some of the other helpful assets may be acquired to some extent with experience and practice, or brought to a high polish if one has something to build on at the beginning. And who has not? As the Arthur Murray ads say, "You, too, can dance!"

After over three decades of being stopped several times a day by people with something on their mind, of having my lapels seized firmly or my sleeve tugged by someone who wants something done that he feels I may be able to do, of long interviews with people with a grievance, a petition, a plan, an invention, or just a two-way ball-bearing tongue, I am ready to maintain against all comers that patience is a prime political virtue. No matter how tired you are, how anxious to get away from it all, how disinterested you would like to let yourself be in the matter now so earnestly being laid on your doorstep, a single flash of irritation may lose you a friend (and some of his friends too) for life.

It is well, in fact it is essential, to remember that no matter how unimportant or undeserving the request for help may seem to you, it is genuinely important, a very real problem to your petitioner. Otherwise, he wouldn't be asking you. It doesn't follow that you can do it. But your being in public life is taken by the public as a sort of holding out that you are on tap to be helpful. If your conduct negates this view, the word goes around that you are a selfish stuffed shirt with no interest in anyone but yourself, and the ill will toward you silently (not so silently!) grows and grows. Some day it may raise its head in political counsels where you are being discussed and the political books are being balanced on you.

Aside from the good you do your own system by exercising restraint and conserving adrenalin, patience is a rewarding political virtue. Not that you should make a doormat of yourself or turn yourself into a servile, cringing dishrag of a man or woman. Not at all. But those who look to you for advice or help have paid you a compliment. They think you can do it. They are entitled to a patient, attentive hearing. That's what you would give them if they came into your drugstore, isn't it? Well, when you're in politics, all the world's your customer. Or so it seems.

Perhaps you cannot do that which you are asked to do. Then an explanation of why you cannot, with the added velvet touch that you wish you could as compared with a brusque "I can't be bothered with that!" will be the difference between having a friend and an enemy. And both friends and enemies seem to grow in politics by geometrical progression.

Not for nothing do the politicians boast of the number of people they have "served." It is comforting assurance to them of the number of friends they have made, of the aura of good will that surrounds their comings and goings and that they hope will attend upon the consummation of their ambitions. Personally, I hate the word. "Serve" seems to carry with it a connotation of servility, which is not really intended in its usage. I much prefer "help," which means what it says. But "serve" has a long start in political usage.

Patience has other merit too. After having done numberless political errands, after considerable work at the polls amid the furor of political campaigns, the pleasure of carrying a spear may well pall on you and your thoughts will turn again to your own sterling qualities. It is high time that they were recognized in some substantial way, which is to say that you think you are overdue for some political office. You may very well be right. But here is where the patience comes in. Your party may not have the positions to offer because they may not be in political power or because "few die and none resign." Or you may not have succeeded as yet in bringing your qualifications and ambitions into the view of those who may be in a position to help you.

How to put yourself into "the way of grace"? The answer to this does not come out of a hat. Go ahead alertly, do superior work at the political level on which you are engaged, and set about knowing better the ward leader and the other political figures who may not know enough about you to have formed an estimate of your qualifications. Take up your political problems with them; let them see what you are doing and what you have accomplished; let them know what your ambitions are; be willing to take on additional responsibility; come up with your ideas for party policy or advancement of party success. Perhaps you can help write party literature or contribute helpful political items to local newspapers or write letters to editors favorable to party colleagues in current controversies. In short, your job is to get to be known as an individual, and an up-and-coming one at that, rather than a political robot. Sounds like the rules for success in any business.

Bear this in mind: When political recognition comes, it usually comes without warning, and you do not know the day, week, or year. But you may have blown your top, your patience exhausted just before the finger of recognition was to uncurl in your direction. You will have had the satisfaction of telling somebody off (probably somebody who will not care too much at that), but you will have tossed away the benefit of all your previous good work by an impatient effort to force someone's hand. Do not hesitate to advance your views with courage and forcefulness, but where do you expect to get with all that yelling?

When you hold public office, if the work you are doing is the sort that comes under public scrutiny, you will need patience to meet the demands that are made upon your time. But these being usually the inevitable concomitants of the job, you will presumably have allowed for them. The greater test of fortitude may come when you are faced with newspaper criticism or attacks from your opponents, which may be biased but which will certainly seem most unjust to you, as none of us are blessed with the faculty of appraising our own actions impartially.

There are, of course, times when statements appearing in newspapers must be answered fully and with candor. But it is the better rule, and followed by most people in public life, that when one is attacked by an unfriendly newspaper or radio commentator, one ignores it. There is a saying: "Never get into an argument with a newspaper or a preacher; the newspaper always has the last word with its readers, and the preacher always calls on Heaven as witness that he is right." Whether this maxim is true or not, most unfriendly attacks from such sources are usually ignored.

In my own experience let me say in all frankness that I have at times gone contrary to this advice, so far as the newspapers are concerned, because I thought (perhaps fatuously) that even an opposition newspaper would portray both sides to its readers if requested to do so. But that very experience leads me to conclude that, by and large, attacks from partisan sources should be ignored. For has not experience been defined as the sum of things we did wrong?

By replying to partisan attacks, you prolong the controversy, call attention to the original unfavorable criticism to those who missed it the first time around, and you multiply the opportunity for unfavorable editorial comments in the press. You have little chance of persuading readers, already conditioned by the policy of their favorite paper, into believing the truth lies

33

on your side of the argument. Also, by replying, you double the publicity and multiply its importance.

If you conclude that I am rather too skeptical about the fairness of some of the opposition press, try it out for yourself sometime if the opportunity offers. Write your letter to the editor and watch what he does to you in the editorial note at the foot of your communication, add that to the title he has put at the top of your letter, and reach for the first-aid kit. Fortunately, there are many fair-minded exceptions to this in the American press and reporters generally are fair and likable; be fair with them and they will be fair with you.

Since the tenor of what I have just written is "do nothing about it," I do not want to leave the subject without suggesting that there are ways to meet unfairness and unwarranted criticism. If the record you make for yourself over a period of years is good, if you have impressed people well, if you have been fair, honorable, and diligent, all this will come to your help when the storms of controversy rage about your head. Those who read about you will ask those who know you what they think of the article in today's paper, and it is what the latter say that will go far to form public opinion about the rightness or wrongness of the act in question. Also, be generous: give reporters all the information you honestly can. Whenever someone I know gets himself or herself talked about, it invariably happens that people say to me, "What do you think about so-and-so?" And whether so-and-so is a so-and-so or not, regard for him goes up or down as his colleagues speak well or ill of him. And this is something every politician knows.

Courtesy is the twin sister of patience; if one is patient, one is likely to be courteous also. Your good politician is as courteous to the well-favored as to the underprivileged. The latter have more votes and very frequently a better sense of citizenship, which it would be wrong to underestimate; also the poor need the protection of wise government most of all. But the former

34

have their points too; they usually hold their citizenship too lightly and often fail to register and vote except during a presidential election. The more often they tell their troubles to their friend in politics, the more likely he is to get them out to vote and the better chance he has to get their support for his candidates or party. And then there comes a day when the chairman of the party finance committee makes up his list. He will not wish to neglect the more plushy citizens. If they have been heard to cry out that "something ought to be done about these terrible conditions!", he will be glad to tell them how they can help.

It is not the easiest thing in the world to be courteous at the polls or in the market place to the gent who tells you in vigorous terms how rotten your party is and why he is going to vote for the other crowd. If he comes at you that way, you aren't going to convince him by high words or by yelling louder than he does although you may amuse the passers-by on an otherwise dull day for them. You may, by such tactics, stir him to such a pitch as to give him the urge to increase his political activity for the opposition. Reflect a minute: why is he so violent in his views? May not this indicate that he feels within himself some lack of security in his beliefs? Perhaps there are inner doubts that courtesy and reason on your part may bring to the surface. It may be that all he is waiting for is for somebody to convince him; he just doesn't want to make it too easy for you. After all, old prejudices die hard. And what can you lose by trying? Honey may cost more than vinegar on Main Street, but on Ballot Boulevard there's no market at all for the sour stuff. Besides, honey is the only known food that won't spoil.

Gregariousness is another definite political asset. While it would not be quite accurate to call it an occupational disease, most politicians have it, and there is an infectious quality about it. It has often been said that the best place to open up

35

a shoe store is on a street where there are a lot of shoe stores, and the best place for a politician is where the people are.

It is no accident that you see a good committeeman or a well-known officeholder around so much. The chances are that he planned it that way. He may appear to have a lot of time on his hands, but he's working all right. He is making his contacts, feeling out sentiment, finding out what you are thinking, trying to learn whether there is any shifting of political winds, looking for "the cloud no bigger than a man's hand" that may forecast some future political tempest. (Rueful note: Sometimes he doesn't see it, even when it's a thunderhead!) This is a part of his political canvass and the better he is, the more time he is apt to devote to it.

Time out for a sermonette: If you want to be as good a citizen as he is a committeeman, tell him what you think about civic affairs, what improvements you think ought to be made, tell him what you expect in candidates for public office, tell him to take a few messages to Garcia for you. You'd be surprised how much gets done—or doesn't get done—by default. *Your* default.

The majority of those who stay in public life any length of time get to be joiners. This comes about, at first, because it is one of the best ways to get to know a lot of people on the basis of association in a common interest or enterprise, but it is cumulative. As one gets to know a lot of people, the opportunities widen, the pressures increase, the desirability of joining this lodge or that order becomes apparent or is made to seem advantageous, and before you know it, the dues are an item! All of which is duly rationalized by the twofold assurance that (a) it is good for your business or profession and (b) advancement comes more readily to one who has wide associations, *i.e.*, "a following."

It is certainly much more than a coincidence that the candidate for mayor or state auditor or governor is usually identified in the public prints as active in lodges, veterans' organizations, church societies, labor unions, chambers of commerce, farm cooperatives, charities, community funds, hospital or alumni groups, or all of them. He knows, and the party leaders and workers who are in his corner know, that this means that Joe Voter is saying to Fanny Franchise, "Do I know him? Why, he's a lodge brother of mine!"

There is no denying that there are some lazy people in politics but not enough in the top layers to dilute seriously the observation that industry and zeal are most important political attributes. To say that one is more likely to succeed if one works hard at it may seem so obvious as not to warrant assertion, but the point should be stressed, if only because wonder is so often expressed at how or why some particular person ever came to hold public office. That such a person may appear to be unfit for the office he holds or may lack zeal in the performance of his public duties is not to say that he was not zealous or industrious in getting the job in the first place or in trying to hold on to it.

It happens more often than otherwise that one who is a competent, hard-working politician is also attentive in the performance of his public duties. As always, it is the exceptions who make the news, the bad news and the good. If unfit (albeit politically zealous) men are put up as candidates for public office, it is primarily the fault of the political party presenting them for the approval of the electorate, and no mistake about it, but let not the voter be self-righteous on that account. It is his fault as well if they get elected. If political parties insist on continually taking "too long a lead off first base," a complacent electorate will let them get away with it; an alert electorate will not.

A comparatively even balance of power between parties often leads to the selection of better candidates. In those cities and counties where the parties have approached something like parity, it is markedly noticeable that there are fewer election frauds and a better choice of qualified candidates. This is an argument against the one-party system in parts of the South and in machine-bossed cities, and what you're thinking is just what I mean to imply. Meanwhile there is solid evidence that a two-party system is on the way in much of the South and the power of big city bosses is notably on the wane.

The odds in favor of an alert electorate are improving. In World War I the average member of the armed forces had finished the sixth grade. In World War II the average GI had completed the second year of high school. Passage of G.I. bills of rights has opened wide the educational doors for veterans. Although education alone is not the answer (the will to do something about one's responsibilities is more to the point), it is an encouraging sign. And the activity of the veterans of our wars in the political affairs of their home towns is notable. Something for the better, civicwise, should come of it.

You cannot get very far in politics, as a general rule, without working pretty hard at it. To know your neighborhood and to help your neighbors is a 365-day-a-year job, as I have said. The man or woman who enters a political campaign a few days before election in opposition to the professional political worker is usually beaten before he or she has started. Sometimes a wave of indignation or reform activity will sweep a group of amateurs to victory, but the day after the election the professional politician is working for the next election, at which time he will usually reverse the verdict. That is, unless the winners have learned that gaining office and holding office are two very different things and have decided to go to work professionally on a 365-day-a-year basis too, which they usually do not.

It is my judgment that if you want to do good work in politics, if you want your industry to have some lasting effect, if you want to see some improvement through the quality of your contribution, you can do the best job by working within the framework of the existing parties or with independent party groups working to improve faulty conditions existing in the party as distinguished from newly formed third parties. Third parties are notoriously unsuccessful and shortwinded in the American political sweepstakes, save in a very few localities (and very rarely nationally), and reform movements usually blow up in a welter of incrimination, inefficiency, and place seeking. One may wish that it were not so, but the record is filled with such noble beginnings and ignoble endings.

In this country, you will find, St. George, that slaying the dragon is an inside job.

The working politician has two strings to his bow; he wants people to have a favorable view of the principles of his party and of its candidates, and he wants to be sure that his neighbors are registered and will vote for the ticket he is working for on election day. The man who likes your product and never comes around to the store for it is not a very good customer. So the main job is to get the vote out on election day. And that takes industry, whether your part in the political pattern is head-quarters work, public speaking, finance, organizing, letter writing or precinct duties at the polls. And the more effective you are, the better results you can show, the greater your political prestige. It has to be actual work and provable results. You can't run a bluff in politics very long. The competition is too keen and the word gets around too quickly.

If, as you go your way in politics, you are blessed with the gift of wit, you are fortunate among men. You are more likely to be born with it than to acquire it. Humor, and an understanding of the uses of humor and its due place, can be developed, as can a warm appreciation of wit in others, but simon-pure wit compares to humor as uranium to pitchblende. Real wit is a rare and radiant thing. A few have possessed it, super-latively, as witness the anecdotes that the names of Chauncey Depew and Al Smith call to mind. Lincoln had it, to etch an issue, to scorch pretension, or to lighten the tragic tension of his time, and so did the late President John F. Kennedy. Gags and topical twists are a dime a dozen but for sterling wit there seem to be few front-rank successors presently on the national scene.

There are, however, many men of humorous flair in politics and their way is easier for it. The Irish seem to have far more than their share of it, and a political speech by a witty Irishman has saved many a gathering from dying on its feet. Other nationalities, likewise, furnish their quota of enlivening wit. If you have it, it will help you. If you haven't, fall back on humor, but don't overdo it. Humor is salt to improve the fare; don't neglect the meat and potatoes. Nothing is so unfunny as the unfortunate who tries to be funny all the time.

A witty passage that will be long remembered by those present occurred when the late Senator Robert Kerr of Oklahoma was described by a Senator of his own party as "great in small things, but small in great things." Without pause for more than an expansive smile, Senator Kerr retorted: "To that slight degree I am ahead of my colleague."

Members of Congress customarily resort to indirect language when putting a fellow member in his place. No one who was there will forget the reverse praise used by Speaker John Mc-Cormack, then Majority Leader) to Representative Clare Hoffman of Michigan that "I hold the gentleman in minimum high regard."

One of the accepted uses of humor is to warm up a gathering, to focus attention on the speaker, to point up the theme you have in mind, as an Irish politician in Philadelphia used to say, "to leave them smiling when you say good-by."

Few qualities can be more favorable to anyone, including the politican, than a sense of proportion, a realization that the great globe itself does not revolve around us. And a well-rounded sense of humor is rarely a part of the psychic luggage of the arrant egotist. Take your work seriously, take your principles seriously, but don't take yourself too seriously. In the cabinet room of the governor of a certain state, there was a sign on the wall so placed that all of the Cabinet members could see it during their session: NO MAN IS INDISPENSABLE. I asked who had put it there and learned that it had been hung by a cabinet officer who had later become so convinced of his indispensability that it had been necessary to fire him.

On various occasions I have heard the remark, "I think I would like politics, but I'm no orator." That shouldn't stop anybody. Most of the men who have made a success of politics, including most of the holders of high office, are no orators. Many of them, by long experience and practice, have become adequate or even excellent public speakers. The accomplished orator is fairly rare (thank Heaven!), and he usually got that way in high school or college. Many of them have perfected one good speech with heavy emotional allusions to Home, Mother, and The Flag, and have been delivering it ever since with suitable minor changes to fit local conditions, of course, and with some added throbbing references to Our Soldier Boys or to the war on poverty.

There are some highly competent orators with the ability to speak inspiringly and effectively on matters of current public interest, who can sway audiences and persuade listeners to their views. They are valuable men to their political parties and are much in demand. But if you can't be an orator, if you can't "pull the cork up in their throats" at least once during the meeting, don't let it bother you. Neither can the vast majority of public speakers. And in the long run you will tot up much more solid and satisfactory results if you speak simply, sincerely, and with conviction on subjects with which you are familiar.

If you feel strongly about your subject, you will probably be able to convey your views to your audience. While listeners may be deeply moved by oratory, an appeal merely to the emotions may not be at all lasting, whereas a logical, tightly reasoned discourse may give them reasons to buttress their views in arguments with others. If you speak with fairness of the opposing viewpoint and conviction as to your own, you may gain adherents to your views who were not with you when you started.

It takes practice, and facility comes with experience. Does it reassure you to learn that a good speaker is nearly always nervous just before he goes to the rostrum? Any person who can talk, can talk in public, of which more at length in another chapter. But don't worry about the orators, except when you have to listen to them.

Another thing, be fair. At all times be fair. Be fair to your friends and your supporters; never let them down when they have given you their backing for any purpose. And above all, be fair to your opponents. Remember what the lawbooks say: a prosecutor may hit hard blows but he must not hit foul ones. Never hesitate to strike out hard, bore into the weakness of your opposition with all legitimate weapons at your command, use all the skill and force you have, make it interesting for the bystanders and tough for your opposition. But keep it clean.

There are times when even the use of the truth can be a blow below the belt. For example, comment on the private life, personal characteristics, or eccentricities of the other fellow may be entirely accurate factually but may have not the slightest connection with the political controversy that pits you in opposition to each other. Resort to that kind of comment may be most unfair. Resist the temptation to strike down another's argument or to derogate from his record by reference to matters for which he should not be held politically answerable, such as the shortcomings of members of his family. Maybe his son was caught in the raid on the Yoo Hoo Casino, but what does it have to do with the merits of your opponent at the next election? Pursue no man to his undeserved hurt.

Resist the temptation, I say, because it will seem to you that voters will often react emotionally to talk such as this, extraneous though it be to the matter at hand. Perhaps they may; perhaps some temporary shift against the other person may seem to result from unfavorable publicity accorded him by virtue of the kind of attack you have launched, but there is a kind of rough balance in these matters which will punish you in the end, rest assured. The voter may get some enjoyment out of the airing of things of this kind, but it is a guilty sort of a kick he gets and he takes it out on you sooner or later. He says you are a mudslinger and he doesn't like this slinging mud. Accordingly, your reputation suffers, and each succeeding presentation of your views is received with less and less credence.

So you see, the argument against unfairness runs along the same lines as the reasons in favor of honesty in politics. It ought to be enough to be honest because honesty is morally right and it ought to be a sufficient argument in favor of fairness and above-the-board dealing that this is morally the only answer. But there is the further evidence, if further evidence you need, that there are sanctions operating to penalize the dishonest, even for acts not within the literal operation of the criminal code. For unfairness, once the public is convinced you are playing that way, it will invoke the penalty against you of loss of trust and confidence. For this sort of thing a Senator from Wisconsin died on stage, long before his physical demise.

Lastly I have reserved one of the most valuable attributes that a man or a woman may have in politics—or out of it for that matter. There is no substitute for courage—neither friendliness, facility of expression, dogged application, guile nor charm. As Lord Bryce said so well, "politicians fail more often through timidity than through rashness." When it is said of one in public life that he will stand up—to use a political phrase—his political courage is worthily praised.

43

Be known as one who will stand up. There is more room on either side of a fence than on it. The view may be better up there, but you aren't getting any place. Timidity is the enemy of progress—your progress.

Granted, you may go through your entire life in politics without taking much of a stand on anything. It is a eunuchoid position and not very gratifying, but you can do it. You will not gain very much respect from anybody; you may not advance very far; or if you do progress from step to step on the political ladder, you will have earned a reputation as you went along as a political Milquetoast or a servile bagman for somebody else. It's a living of a sort but not much more can be said for it.

Plenty of opportunities for a showing of courage will arise in a political career. There will be times when you will have a choice between standing by your friends and allies when you are in what seems to be a losing fight or of leaping upon the bandwagon of the opposition. This may occur in a primary fight in your own party or in a general election campaign between the two parties. Or it may involve some realignment on matters of party policy. What are you going to do about it besides sweat blood? Are you going down to defeat for what you believe in, or are you going to jump to the lads who look like the winners? This kind of political trapeze work will get you a ticket to the victory ball if you switch over; it will also lift a lot of eyebrows in both camps. Therefore, the making of this kind of decision may not always involve true courage; it may be no more than expediency. But you will find that it does take courage to keep on sticking by the loser or to resist offers of advancement from the other side in return for your support. It takes courage, too, to continue to fight for your beliefs when they seem to be growing more and more unpopular, when you find yourself a member of an ever-shrinking minority.

If you hold some public office, your courage will be tested at times if it happens that some politically powerful figure asks you to do something that you should not do. The more you are known as a man of integrity the less likely this is to happen and the easier it is to handle if it does happen.

The wise politician prefers to deal with honest officials. For one who would double cross another for him on this occasion would double cross him on another. Impropriety in dealing with public officials happens less often than the general public thinks. Again, the exceptions make the news. But it can happen and it does at times. That is when you will have your chance to decide whether you are a man or a mouse. I should make an observation right here on how to handle a situation of this kind. You have already decided that you must decline to do that which has been suggested. If you reject the proposal with a roar of injured innocence, do you know what your visitor is going to think? He is going to conclude that he has not made his offer attractive enough to you, whereupon he may retire to ponder whether to return later with a better proposal or to try someone else. In short, he thinks you protest too much; he is not convinced of your sincerity. The Bible says, "The righteous are as brave as a lion." But it is not implied that the righteous should *sound* like Leo at feeding time.

Whenever it is necessary to say no, it is desirable to give a good reason. Is it not better to tell your visitor, who may or may not know why this request is improper, just why you cannot do what he asks? Tell him reasonably and tactfully. Then when he leaves you he knows exactly where he stands. He may be considerably aggrieved for all your tact, but his opinion of you has gone up. And you are not likely to hear that kind of proposal from him again.

I said that impropriety in dealing with public officials happens less often than the public thinks. There is so much skepticism about this that perhaps a certain amount of documentation is in order. I have held appointive or elective public office for over forty years. During all of that time only twice were definitely improper proposals made to me, one of them from a bail bonds-man and one from a lawyer, since disbarred. Not once has any person active in political life proposed an improper or off-color procedure. And in many meetings with my colleagues holding the same type of office, I have found that their experience has been much the same as mine. I suggest that you check this for yourself. Talk to some officeholders with whom you are acquainted. Ask their opinion on this. If you think their answer about themselves is a foregone conclusion, ask them about some other officeholders or about public officials generally, even of the opposite political party. I think you will find that the con-sensus is that, while political leaders have a strong interest in having a say about who holds public office, these same leaders have a code of their own about not interfering with the per-formance of public duties. It is not unusual to hear a politician say, "I put him up for that job, and I've never asked him to do a thing for me that he couldn't properly do for anybody else."

I have another occasion in mind that also calls for the exercise of courage. Your performance of your duties as a public of-ficial may come in for criticism. It may develop that your actions have become exceedingly unpopular. Examine the criticism; there may be merit in it. If you have been wrong, have the courage to say so and to reverse your course of conduct. If you are fully convinced you are right, then stick to your guns. Again, tact helps. Take the opportunity to explain why you are doing what you are and be reasonable in meeting your critics. You may disarm them. Or you may have to battle it out. One officeholder, harassed by the wealthy members of a community who were enraged over changes in a zoning ordinance, com-mented, "I told my men, 'Damn the Tuxedos! Go ahead!' "

So I have set down here quite a catalogue of the traits, the assets, of a successful practitioner of the political art. Then why, you ask, are politicians held in such low esteem? Some possible reasons, not all-inclusive, occur to me as I write. I think the first and most obvious answer is because so many fail to attain the ideal of what a good politician should be. So many other men and women fall short as good businessmen, housewives, architects or roofers. Yet one does not hear that "architecture is a dirty business" or "roofing is a dirty business." Yet who has failed to say, at some time or another, "politics is a dirty business"?

This suggests the second part of the answer: It is inherent in their calling that men in the public eye should be subjected to more criticism than others. The public remedy for dealing with businessmen or roofers it doesn't like is to go to other businessmen or other roofers. The whole process of doing something about politicians it doesn't like seems to the public to have something mysterious, something arcane, about it. There seem to be so many road blocks and so much delay in the way of remedying an unsatisfactory political situation that the people take refuge from their distress and bewilderment by irritably dismissing the subject with "Politics is a dirty business, anyway."

The recourse open to them in business, that is taking their trade to a more satisfactory competitor, does not seem to work the same way in politics. The public reaction to that method is apt to be, "But the other party isn't any better!" There is a remedy, but it involves putting Mr. and Mrs. Average Citizen to more trouble than ordinarily they wish to take. Politics can be improved the same way automobiles and refrigerators were improved, by an insistent public demand for those improvements. That is, by an insistence on the part of the public that the public business be conducted by better-qualified people, that better candidates be offered for the voter's choice. But the voter often lets the primary election, where he might exert his right to a selection of candidates, go by default. At the general election the party choices are presented to him, and if he doesn't like either candidate, he doesn't blame himself. He is apt to say, "One party is as bad as another."

It is also true that the faults of politicians (as of other men) are more newsworthy than their virtues. There is no news in forty years of faithful public service. There is plenty when Politician Takes Contract Bribe; that's on the front pages with Banker Caught in Love Nest.

Before Aristophanes wrote *The Birds* or Plato his *Republic*, criticism of men in public office was, as it is now and probably will always be, an outlet for John Q. Public's dissatisfaction with things as they are in an imperfect world; he feels the wounds of taxes yet cannot spy who wields the sword. His feeling that nothing can be done about it contributes to his *Weltschmerz*. And this critical attitude is a good thing. Every so often it cumulates into action, and even when it goes no further than talk, it serves to remind the holder of the public trust that he is under the people's eye.

Lastly, there is another reason why politicians seem to be held in such low esteem—we have to support them!

5. Do's and Don'ts of Politics

THE first "don't" had better be: Don't expect to find anywhere a comprehensive catalogue of these. They will, for the most part, arise from your own experience. The main thing is to be on the lookout for them and to profit accordingly. Learn from your mistakes, and don't think you won't make them! But it is a sign of growth in wisdom when you find that you are making different mistakes, not just duplicating the old ones. As the Chinese say, "Fool me once, shame on you; fool me twice, shame on me."

Also, learn from other people's mistakes. They will keep you supplied with plenty of source material if you aren't making your own fast enough.

The most anyone else can do for you is to drop some hints born of one's own experience, which may be of value to the next traveler along that road. As in any other walk of life, if you seek information of practical and practicing politicians, you will find that it is freely offered to any willing listener. If you have ever incautiously asked your neighbor what to do about a cold in the head, you know what I mean.

Right off the bat, here's a good "do" for you; know what you want from a career in politics. Why do you think you would like being in public affairs, where do you want to go politically, and what use do you expect to make of your opportunities? What kind of qualifications are needed for the race you want to run; do you have them and, if not, are they the kind which you believe you can acquire? Are you willing to put in the time and effort, knowing that both may be considerable?

HOW TO RUN FOR PUBLIC OFFICE, AND WIN!

In other words, *plan!* There are as inescapable reasons for blueprints in politics as in building a house, and a plan of operation is as logical in laying out your political campaign as in a military maneuver. Unless you know the kind of public position you are seeking, you will be operating more or less in a vacuum no matter how zealously you have worked. The right man is found in the right place (more often than you might think) because that is where he meant to be.

Assuming that you know where you want to go in political life and that your plans include holding public office, how do you go about it? We have already discussed what a political organization is like and how the beginner makes his start there. I hope that I may have been able to make the political cosmos seem less mysterious to you.

Have in mind the kind of work you can do. Find out what jobs in the city, county, state, or federal government there are of the type you have in mind, whether or not they come under civil service, and if not, who has the appointive power. It is not a bad idea to let your ambitions be known to the political leader in your community. Enlist his interest, if you can, so that when a vacancy occurs you may be able to have him urge your selection for the place. If you get it, well and good. If not, accept the situation with good sportsmanship; it will enhance your chances the next time.

At all times in your political activities do be cooperative and helpful to as many people as occasion brings your way. One of the greatest assets you can have is friends—and lots of them. The more friends you have in the right places the greater the interest in your success and advancement. If you are rewarded with recognition, the more friends and well-wishers you have, the more people (that is to say, potential voters) will be pleased to hear of your good fortune. While this redounds to your credit, it also creates good will toward your political party, a fact of which the political leaders were not unaware when they compared your qualifications and your following with those of other aspirants for the same place.

Needless to say, the kind of friends you make will have a considerable bearing on your political future. If they are a credit to you, it is a fair inference that you must have done something to merit their regard.

One of my associates often comments, "A man seems to make two different kinds of friends—active and passive." The latter may well meet the classic definition of a friend as one who knows all your faults and likes you still; he may harbor the warmest and most amiable regard, but he will pass up one opportunity after another to perform some service in your behalf simply because it never occurs to him that he has been presented with such an opportunity. On the other hand, the active friend— ah, there's the man for you—will be as alert as radar to detect those occasions where a word to someone else or a timely suggestion to you may set in motion a train of events on which you can ride to your predetermined destination. Fortunately for all of us, a great many men and women seem to have the quality of active friendship. Who among us would not prefer the posy passed by hand to the imposing wreath delivered to the graveside?

While it is most important to one engaged in politics not to let the low, descending sun find him without some deed of kindness done, it is almost equally important not to throw into the face of your beneficiary the fact of your having been of service to him. "To remind the man of the good turns you have done him is very much like a reproach," says Demosthenes, himself no slouch as an experienced public man. There are ways to get him out to the polls and do not neglect them, but if you tax him with the recollection of past services, he may vote the other way just to spite you for your lack of tact—a sad thing but true.

Disraeli, whose long career as a leader of a political party in Great Britain knew many ups and downs, commented once that "there is no gambling like politics." Well, naturally. Because politics is people. So study people. Learn all you can about their aspirations and desires, what they think about, what makes them tick. Understand their approaches to their major preoccupations: how to make a living and how to be reasonably happy.

Henry Adams says, in *The Education of Henry Adams*, "Knowledge of human nature is the beginning and end of political education." Your clinical material is all around you; learn to evaluate the difference between the casual reaction of the moment and the more deeply held conviction. Thread the mazes of bias and prejudice; learn how to deal with (and to heal where you can) the running sores of bigotry and intolerance. Getting along with people takes a lifetime of doing, but the politician has to know how to get along with more people more of the time than almost anyone except girls at the information booth at the airport.

Learn to remember names and faces. As a matter of practice, consciously charge your mind to associate names with personal characteristics and the circumstances of the meeting. People like it. You will live a long time before you meet anyone who is not flattered to know that you not only remember his or her name but also where you met and what you talked about. And not to remember unfortunately carries with it at least a trace of inference that you did not regard the prior meeting as worth remembering. Our sense of our own importance is such that we cannot accept such an implication with equanimity.

It is especially flattering to discover, on meeting after a long interval, that what you said on the other occasion was marked, noted, and inwardly digested. I know a politician in West Virginia who jots in a little pocket notebook the kernel of any conversation he has had with a constituent. Imagine the latter's pleasure on receiving a letter a year or so later, beginning "I recall how interesting and helpful to me were the views you expressed on the —— situation in ——, during our conversation in Smith's Restaurant in May 1966."

And speaking of letters, if your political activities involve correspondence, be sure, very sure, to answer every letter you get, and if you can answer them within twenty-four hours of their receipt, so much the better. People who are unused to writing letters about matters political (and some who are used to it) are inclined to be skeptical about the results. You will surprise them pleasantly by your promptness in replying and even more pleasantly if you show by your answer that you have given careful and conscientious thought to what the writer had to say. Scan the letter carefully to find that part of it with which you can agree, and early in your reply assure your correspondent of your agreement with him in that particular. Thus, if there are parts of the letter with which you cannot agree or requests with which you cannot comply, you have softened the impact. Your use of tact has not compromised the convictions you hold, nor have you misled him by promising to do that which you cannot undertake, but you may win his everlasting friendship by the thoughtful and courteous content of your answer. And you might close by inviting your correspondent to write you again, whenever he has something on his mind, or invite him to come to see you. He may be disappointed that he has not gotten what he wanted or he may continue to differ with you on the subject matter discussed, but he can hardly help being complimented by the consideration with which you treated his suggestions and your recognition of the dignity of his opinion. And he certainly cannot say, "I wrote to that fellow and the so-and-so didn't even answer my letter!"

One more thing: if to comply with a request may take days or weeks, write at once to acknowledge the letter and assure the writer that work on his problem is in progress.

53

I know a very distinguished gentleman from a border state who had represented his constituency in the national legislature for more than a generation. It was his unfailing rule to close all of his letters, whether in answer to complimentary, uncomplimentary, or routine correspondence, with the words: "I am, your friend, A—— W——." He told me that he often encountered constituents on visits home, who hauled out of their pockets dog-eared letters from him, often years old, and pointed pridefully to that concluding line. And consider what Franklin Roosevelt was able to accomplish with "my friends . . ."!

I think another good rule of thumb is: Don't violate Rule Six. Freshmen members of the U.S. Senate and House of Representatives hear this adjuration from an older member not long after they are sworn in. As is natural, they ask, "But what is Rule Six?" and are promptly told, "Rule Six is—don't take yourself too seriously." "Then what are Rules One, Two, Three, Four, and Five?" At which point they learn the answer which, if they are wise, they never forget. "Why, they are all the same—just don't take yourself too blamed seriously!" In other words, wherever you find yourself, whatever you do, keep a saving sense of proportion. No matter what your job is, you can always learn from someone else with greater experience, and the more seriously you take yourself the less seriously others may come to take you. Until finally the voters come to take you away to a well-deserved rest in electoral retirement.

This is not to say that you should not take seriously the duties of whatever position you fill, that you should not approach soberly the requirements of your office. Woodrow Wilson said of public officials, "Some people grow in public office; others swell." Growth is salutary but, as you know, most swellings are painful.

While you are restraining your public life within the bounds of a due sense of proportion, you will be well advised to keep your personal life above criticism. It is good judgment as well as good morals to remember that reference to "The Honorable Mr. ———" brings derisive smiles when it is not exactly descriptive.

We Americans are notably good teamworkers. Politics, like other organized efforts involving the energies of aggregations of people, calls for close teamwork. One of the principal reasons our political system has continued for so long as a two-party affair lies in our tendency to choose up sides and to align ourselves either with a winning combination or with one that we believe can become a winning combination. In our preference for games we turn out the biggest crowds for the contest between two well-trained teams, as in football and baseball. The European political system of countless blocs scrabbling for control through ever-changing coalitions is not for us. The fact that the laws of many states tend to perpetuate the two-party system is the result, rather than the cause, of our American preference for a contest between two rather clearly defined organized units. It is interesting to note, in this connection, that a survey in the South, where one party was for so long a time dominant over the other, reveals that a large majority of the persons questioned held the opinion that two evenly balanced political parties would be better for their region. The voter suspects that competition is as good for government as it is for trade.

So it is well to recognize the importance of teamwork in politics and to evaluate your status as a member of the team. Political victory is gained only through the concerted efforts of all the workers throughout the political organization. They cannot win without your efforts and the efforts of many others like you, and you cannot win alone. It is one of those "who won the war?" situations all over again.

If you hold a political office, be it elective or appointive, you are there because of the detailed, continuous unspectacular work of a lot of different hard workers who brought success to your party. And unless the nature of the position you hold precludes by law or consideration of propriety your further participation in politics, you will be expected to continue to assist by every means within your power the advancement of the fortunes of your party and your teammates to the extent consistent with your personal integrity. Forget this, and you will learn in time that the name of a political ingrate is known from Gath to Beersheba (*i.e.*, from the first ward to the county chairman).

And, akin to the importance of answering letters is another adjuration—*keep the engagements you make.* You may often be able to avoid engagements that are undesirable to make or difficult to keep, but once they are made, be sure to be there if it is humanly possible. There may be times when you are compelled to cancel an engagement to appear or to speak at a meeting, but your nonattendance furnishes opportunity for comment and not all of it may be favorable. It may be necessary to accept an invitation, conditioned upon the happening or not happening of a particular conflicting event, but if this is done, your reason for conditional acceptance should be clearly stated. Make sure that it is well understood at the time. If you must refuse to appear before a group whom you would like to meet or to know better, you can usually leave the door open for a later invitation, and if you think the suggestion would be favorably received, you can perhaps suggest the name of a substitute at the meeting to which you have been invited. In any event, send a wire or message with the request that it be read for you at the meeting.

Because of the constantly increasing Congressional work load, members of Congress have frequently utilized telephone hookups to speak with an audience back home when they have been unavoidably detained. There are several advantages: this way the legislator shows that he cares about his audience and is doing all that he can to communicate with them. Moreover, the talk by telephone finds him hard at work, a fact which sometimes unnerves the efforts of a potential opponent who may also be speaking before the group. I have found that when the hookup is directly from the cloakroom and is even interrupted to rush out, vote and return, the effect is dramatic enough to be rewarding. If there is time, a filmed greeting can be made and sent, if the size of the group warrants it.

There is another—if slightly unworthy—advantage to the telephone hookup. You don't have to stand still for the question period.

And now for a series of miscellaneous don'ts:

Don't lose your temper. "Loss of temper is a loss of power." Also, it leads you into thoughtless word and careless act, which you are pretty certain to regret later. When you lose your temper you give yourself away; it becomes apparent that you are not too sure of the reasonableness of your position. The Chinese say, "Keep your head cool, your feet warm and your eyes open." Anything wrong with that advice?

Don't hit below the belt. The public is the referee in political bouts, and they will call the fouls on you. So an attempt to take a doubtful or unfair advantage of your opponent will react against you. In the same category comes mudslinging. Avoid it. As to what is, or is not, mudslinging, the public is not always sure. They are inclined to think that any hard blow struck at your opponent that tends to put him in a bad light may be mudslinging, especially if your opposition claims that it is. If your attack is just and on the level, do not be deterred solely on this account but have the public's attitude in mind and be sure that you present your charges in such a way as to answer any criticism on this score.

You can always make clear the differentiation between mere personalities and fair comment on the effect of the public acts and views of one seeking or holding public office, for which your opponent must accept responsibility if he seeks to gain or hold a position of public trust. Let me illustrate: To charge that one is an associate of heavy drinkers descends to personalities; it would be called mudslinging. But to charge (if it is a fact) that the county treasurer employs clerks who wander drunkenly around at their work is fair comment, if provable, because it reflects on your opponent's conduct of his public office. You have every right to point out that to permit that kind of conduct argues unfitness for the office he holds.

Don't be diverted from your target, but don't strike him while his back is turned.

Don't fall for flattery. The flatterer wants something, and it is probable that you are the person he has in mind to help him get it. Flattery is hard to resist, because the picture the flatterer paints is so often similar to one's self-portrait. It is the easiest of all weapons to use and so often effective. Better make up your mind to get well acquainted with the motives of such a person before you allow his surface geniality and generous appraisal of your talents to pull your guard down.

Don't be thin-skinned either. "Censure is the tax a man pays to the public for being eminent," said Jonathan Swift. And there is always the chance that your critic is right.

Don't underestimate your opponent. You are not only up against him; you are up against his friends too. And some of them may be quite resourceful. It is better for you if he underestimates you. It is better for *his* guard to be down than yours.

Never build up, *i.e.*, overpublicize, your adversary. Some candidates for public office never mention their opponents by name. What you want people to remember is *your* name, the party ticket *you* are running on, the things *you* stand for. Every time you make a statement that appears in the paper, if you mention your opponent's name, you have shared the publicity with him. The voter, when he enters the voting booth, is confronted with a long list of names, most of which, in all probability are unfamiliar to him. He is likely to vote for a name he recognizes. Hence, it is your name you are trying to get before him, and if he has never heard of your opponent, should you complain of that?

And don't mix into a squabble when two or more of your political adversaries are at it hammer and tongs. You have nothing whatever to gain by declaring yourself in, and by staying out you may benefit from their mutual exposure of each other's shortcomings. As the Arab proverb has it, "When the wind fans your fire, don't waste your breath." We lawyers say, "When the court is with you, keep quiet."

Don't overdo cordiality in meeting people. That is, don't be overeffusive in praise or promises. You may be regarded as a little too ripe for public consumption. Artemus Ward, the Will Rogers of his day, used to say, "The prevailin' weakness of most public men is to slop over. G. Washington never slopt over."

Don't sound off unless you are sure of your facts. Don't rush in ahead of the angels. *Think!* You can spend a lot of unproductive time later, explaining why you never meant what you said. Better be right the first time.

Don't be extreme in dress or mannerisms, unless you are running for court jester.

Don't make promises you can't keep. Broken promises are remembered longer than kept ones.

Don't bluff! Sooner or later, you will be caught at it and all of your previous actions, even the sincere ones, will be subject to considerable discount. Better follow Mark Twain's lead: "I was gratified to be able to answer promptly, and I did. I said I didn't know."

And don't be late for the meeting. They may be talking about you!

6. What Is Public Opinion?

> *That mysterious independent variable*
> *of political calculation, Public Opinion.*
>
> —T. H. HUXLEY.

PUBLIC opinion is private opinion on the loose. It is what you think multiplied by all the other people who are thinking about the same thing. Jan Struther said, in *A Pocketful of Pebbles:*

> Private opinion creates public opinion. Public opinion overflows eventually into national behavior and national behavior, as things are arranged at present, can make or mar the world. That is why private opinion, and private behavior, and private conversation are so terrifyingly important.

Miss Struther hit the tack with the hammer. Most of us have little realization of the extent to which we, as individuals, are the constructors of public opinion. But the communication of one person's opinion to another, and by that other to still another, generates a sort of chain reaction that billows up from the nation's street corners and gathering places and is swept by teletype and airwave to all the nation's people, whereupon the process repeats itself until public interest veers to some other matter. The kind of thing that alarmed Miss Struther, I imagine, was the thoughtless or rather the unthinking repetition of pat phrases of enmity or dislike toward some other nation or race, which grows in time into a deadly phobia. The resulting war thus became an "inevitable conflict" between traditional enemies.

When some new idea, development or controversy hits the headlines, public reaction has not yet been hardened by prejudice or shaped by the interaction of other opinion. There is an interval when the state of flux is so thick you could cut it with a knife—or mold it with a timely point of view. Here is the maximum opportunity for the makers and shapers of public opinion.

The way in which public opinion gets things done was first impressed on me some years ago when I was engaged in a grand jury investigation for the prosecutor's office. During the fifteen months' duration of the investigation (probably a record in the length of time and number of witnesses examined by a grand jury) it was the usual procedure for the jury to examine witnesses daily along lines suggested either by members of the grand jury or by the district attorney's office, following the main thread of the investigation as discussed in the original charge of the presiding judge. But how did the suggested lines of investigation get into the minds of the jurors or the prosecutors?

Each morning on entering the jury room, I noticed that the jurors were reading and discussing the news reports and editorials on their previous day's doings. The members of the district attorney's staff had read the same reports and commentary. Parenthetically, in many states, trial or petit jurors are not permitted to read news articles pertaining to their duties during the trial; this restriction is not usually applied to grand jurors, whose duties include the finding of indictments and investigations into the conduct of county, city, or federal affairs.

The day's work with the grand jury usually began with a general discussion that invariably included consideration of any suggestions for new lines of inquiry which had appeared in the papers. The county's newspapers were thus able to influence the course of the investigation and to light up various avenues of inquiry. When the public's interest finally flagged, the newspapers undertook to convince the jurors that their work was over. As it happened, this jury was in session during a period of business depression. They were getting two meals a day in addition to their pay, and they were not especially anxious to shut up shop. For a time the jury ignored the hints, but the presiding judge took cognizance of them. The jury went down to one free meal a day. Still the sessions continued. So the judge's next step was to decree no more meals at the public expense. While all this was going on, the jurors were reading in their papers such headlines as Jury Reports Shortly and Grand Jury Nears End. So the grand jury prepared its presentment and went home.

In the speaker's lobby of the U.S. House of Representatives there are racks of current newspapers arranged according to geographical sections of the country. Before each day's session this is a good place to see public opinion at work. Your congressman, having already read at breakfast the Washington viewpoint on legislative and executive happenings, is now engrossed in a careful examination of editorial comment and letters to the editor in the journals published in his congressional district. He wants to know how he is doing and what he might well be doing according to the folks at home. He is analyzing public opinion; his actions will be influenced accordingly.

The vast majority of people look about them for some source of help in forming their judgments or buttressing their attitude toward a given happening. Necessarily we cannot be expected to be experts or pundits save perhaps within the narrow limits of our own experience. What is more natural than to exchange views with whoever is available and, better still, if opportunity offers, to absorb, embrace, and present as our own the lofty dogma of the commentator? But are we formulating principles or assembling prejudices?

Have you not at times had the amusing experience of hearing two of your friends earnestly elucidating for each other the inner portent of some current to-do, their conversation revealing the common source of their information? Perhaps you yourself realized that they were mentally taking in each other's washing, because your own slant had been formed by reading the same columnist or hearing the same broadcaster.

As Samuel Butler wrote, in *The Art of Propagating Opinion,* "The public buys its opinions as it buys its meats, or takes in its milk, on the principle that it is cheaper to do this than to keep a cow. So it is, but the milk is more likely to be watered."

After all, in this day of syndication and commentators, are we not in danger of reverting to a sort of tribal system where we shall split up into warring sects of Huntley-Brinkleyites, Evans-Novakites, Pearsonists, or something known as a Harry Reasoner. The devotion of millions of people to their favorite prophet of the press or television is not very cheering to the hopeful idealist who would like to see the day come when people reason things out for themselves firsthand. Has there ever been such a day? Will there ever be?

"He is very influential." "She has quite a following." When applied to public figures, what is meant by this? Does it not mean that what such a person does or says will influence the thoughts and actions of others? When the something new we were talking about hits the headlines or the TV screen, the media hasten to get quotes about it from influential people and, reading these offerings, the public begins to take sides, more and more influential people are quoted, and the issue takes shape. Incidentally, many a minor event has been deliberately blown up into a raging debate by this use of quotations and counter-quotations or sensational TV shots. It is most apt to occur when the news intake over the city desk is a little slow and the news needs to be hopped up. And sometimes these controversies are contrived by politicians trying to create interest in a flagging political campaign or by somebody's press agent grinding axes at so much per ax.

Political parties and working politicians are aware that public opinion isn't something that "just grew" like Topsy. They know that public opinion grows from private opinion and that it is often created by expert reportorial work or by the making of favorable news at the right time or by highlighting developments unfavorable to the opposition. Every political reporter gets more news releases handed to him than he can use, although he uses as many as he can justify. The same sources that gave the news releases can often be counted on for tips or news slants or valuable background material for special stories. And the reporter protects his sources of material. Very rarely indeed will any newspaperman use information given to him in confidence, that is he will not "leak" the story for a scoop.

Some politicians fight shy of the press. When they say, "No comment," they mean it. But one who is, or expects to be, a candidate for an elective office will do well to let the people of his city, county, or state hear something of him and that, favorable.

As not everyone seems to know, there are two kinds of publicity. The bad kind can often be very bad indeed for your future prospects as an aspiring public servant. There is quite a difference between being noted and being notorious. A few politicians have capitalized on buffoonery, which may lead you to believe that there may be profit in making a public fool of yourself. Better wait. The people you are thinking of did. As a rule they had reached positions of considerable political power before they began playing for the laughs. Huey Long had become the ruthless dictator of Louisiana years before he made headlines with his recipes for "pot likker" on the Senate floor. The Little Flower (the late Mayor LaGuardia) had a long record of public service in Washington and New York before he took to reading the Sunday comics over the radio. If there is a moral here, it is that there's no fool like a young fool.

How can you help yourself with good publicity? Handing in

avowedly political press releases (in which your name figures more or less prominently) to the papers will not prove successful. However, as you take greater interest in civic affairs—become an officer of charitable or community projects or put in an appearance as a taxpayer on a proposal before your local governing body—some of your efforts will prove to be newsworthy. Your name will appear more often as you become active and influential.

If you are holding some elective office or an appointive office, you will have more frequent opportunity to make news or to figure in the news reports of the day if your duties are such as to bring you into the public purview. A proposal or endorsement by you of a city or county improvement will have news value because you are a selectman or town counsel or city architect. In other words, you may be in a position to do something about it and the public is interested in your ideas. You are now engaged in shaping public opinion whether you have thought of it that way or not. It also follows that if you are an officeholder, you may not have to wait for news to happen in your department. You can call in the reporters and make some. Tell them about the proposed improvements at the fair grounds and why the gambling concessions will not be allowed to operate, or tell them why you think the tax rate ought to be reduced. But don't go in for braggadocio, and don't sound off too much. Remember that the lad who yelled wolf too often didn't get much help the last time around. It could happen to you.

If you are a candidate, not yet in office, you can make news too. It may be more difficult because you can't say what you can do about it as an officeholder, but you can say what ought to be done and what you will do if elected. If your ideas are good, well-presented and attention-demanding in content, you will get them highlighted by press, radio and television. More will be said hereafter about the operation on radio and television of established doctrines designed to balance the handling of statements by contestants for the same office.

An old reliable method of getting publicity is the letter to the editor from you or one of your supporters. He may publish it; that depends on how topical it is and how interesting you make it. It also depends on how much interest there is in the subject that leads you or your friend to take pen in hand. If it is favorable publicity you want, don't be too obvious. Bear in mind that the editor will not be publishing the screed because it is important to you but because he thinks it may be interesting to his readers.

Letters to the editor often play quite a part in political campaigns. Workers at party campaign headquarters, labor union political workers, and pressure groups for this and that at times deluge the editorial department, particularly during the heat of an election contest. All of them know that this part of the editorial page is closely scanned by candidates and public officials.

Radio and television are now regarded as essential in the great game of molding public opinion. The effectiveness of the average quarter-hour political speech is open to some doubt. No one since President Roosevelt has shown his mastery of radio techniques as a means of persuasion.

On the other hand, I think there is something to be said for TV forums. There the atmosphere of the town hall is recreated, tempers flash, humor darts in and out, interest is maintained, and discussion of the subject continues in the living room or next day at the restaurant. Also, public figures under the stress of debate often reveal new facets of their personality and become better known, favorably or otherwise. More will be said on debates in the next chapter.

Consider the use of "spot time" in TV and radio for political purposes. There are the little fifteen-second, thirty-second or one-minute announcements in which the merits of a party or candidate are enumerated in tabloid form or presented in brief dramatic skits, often set to a repetitive musical theme. The usefulness of these spot announcements lies in their comparative inexpensiveness (yet still costly) in that they call for a very short concentration of attention on the part of the listener (being therefore less likely to be turned off), and their message, by repetition, may seep into the consciousness of the housewife as she does the ironing or of the paterfamilias halfway through the evening paper. If properly timed and professionally prepared, they can play a most important part in a compaign to get the voter registered, to get him to vote on election day, and to get him to vote your way.

Political parties also use the TV or radio for full-dress speeches by party bigwigs, for interviews on political subjects, for straight news events, for broadcasts of interest to special groups, such as veterans, young people, farmers, minority groups, etc., for biographical sketches and five-minute pep talks, all of these with or without music.

However, since TV and radio stations are to be licensed in the "public interest," they are required by the Federal Communications Commission to make available an equitable amount of time to candidates and to public service programs. These may take the form of debates or forums presenting differing points of view on the same program or the granting of equal amounts of time to speakers of opposing points of view politically. They also consist of political or civic educational programs presented straight or dramatized or of interviews with national, state, or local officials.

Another way to influence public opinion by getting your name and views before the voters is to have a friend comment favorably in the press or on the many television and radio shows in each area which encourage the viewer to get something off his chest. If you enjoy an alert opposition, they may turn this against you by taking similar advantage of this free 'natural' resource.

Do not overlook the impact of radio in our expanding and more affluent urban society where so many drivers are listening in their cars as they while away traffic delays or even to hand portables during intervals in sports events. Remember, too, the kids carrying transistors. Someday they will vote!

There is much room for argument as to which is more effective—newspaper, TV or radio publicity—and how and to what extent each should be used. The extent of nourishment in the budget of the campaign finance committee usually determines the scope of the program evolved. After deciding on the amount to be spent on TV and radio and the form of presentation of your material, the party or candidate's TV-radio director or advertising agent will make contact with the TV and radio stations and work out the plans and time allocations in detail. Your finance committee will have to raise the money and pay it in advance!

The main thing is to keep it short and to keep it interesting, and to bear in mind that what you are trying to do is to persuade the listener to your point of view.

Of course, the problem, as always in TV and radio, is how to keep the viewer-listener watching and listening.

7. Public Relations
(In Political Campaigns)

YOUR public relations depend, in the first instance, upon your personal attributes and relationships. But professional image-makers can improve and enhance the persuasiveness of political candidates. They are paid to get results and since they stay in business, it follows reasonably that they have met with some success. The public relations man ought to be a professional, and if he is going to be objective, he shouldn't have any ax to grind but his employer's.

A public relations man who expects to get a political job out of his work for you has already forfeited some of his political independence because he is unable to talk like a Dutch uncle. He is limited in giving you the bad news, and the desire to please is apt to fog up his obligation to inform. Therefore, your public relations man should be an expert, a professional, and not beholden to you except on a contractual basis. He should, of course, be someone in whom you can place full trust and confidence because he will need to know more things about you than your mother does.

By all means, consult with and retain paid professional public relations and advertising consultants if you can. They have much to tell you and many ways to help. Your opponent will almost certainly use the same sort of campaign assistance.

Arthur Peterson says: "The ability of citizens to understand the major issues of public policy confronting them; to discuss and to reach decisions regarding these issues have been the articles of faith that lie at the center of the American experiment in popular government.

"The function of political public relations is obviously to provide a favorable climate for one's own party and to assist in the development of an unfavorable climate for the opposition party and its candidates. Ideally the public relations man does this without doing violence to the concept of an informed rational electorate. Quite to the contrary, political public relations in its best sense stimulates and participates in government on the basis of enlightened discussion and meaningful choice at the polls. In other words, responsible public relations means more than the 'engineering of consent.' "[1]

It is nevertheless obvious that a pleasant personality is easier to sell than its pallid counterpart; gregariousness means better cooperation in the common effort than is afforded by one who loves his privacy. Tact sells better than bluntness. A reputation for getting things done and working harmoniously with others is, if not half the battle, at least a head start.

Here we will, of necessity, be discussing public relations in more general terms than you will with your campaign advisers. Each campaign for every office differs from another in the weight to be given various campaign techniques, in the degree to which the candidate does or does not carry the major burden of the campaign, in the funds available for use by the communications media, in the economic, political, ethnic and geographic nature of the constituency. The nature of the opposition also affects the scope of the problem and the course of the campaign.

This discussion then will consider the broad aspects of the public relations job to be done, with some guidelines and suggestions such as the way in which the different media may be employed, in proportion to their effective reach.

The chairman of a national party recently asserted that 39% of the people depend on radio as their chief source of news.

---

[1] Dr. Arthur Peterson, "Section II", *Republican Victories Through Public Relations* (Washington, D. C.: Republican National Committee, 1966), p. 4.

Nearly all homes today contain more than one radio. In rural areas the percent of persons depending on radio as their prime source of news is probably higher.

Radio has the advantage of repetition over newspapers, which carry a story only once. Therefore, many readers will miss it altogether. Properly planned, your statement, if newsworthy, can make it on the noon broadcast, the 6 or 7 p.m. news and the 11 p.m. roundup. In some cities there are stations which broadcast nothing but news at all times. Their captive audience includes those thousands of motorists fighting heavy traffic, particularly on urban and suburban highways. Here you will get the important repetition I mentioned in another chapter.

Your professional adviser will know how best to service radio stations but there are several commonly used methods: For example, tape recordings mailed to all stations, or you can record a statement once (even on the campaign trail) and your aides can use the recording (made on the spot or over the telephone) over and over. They can call one or a number of stations which might broadcast the material "live" for immediate use or tape it themselves for news programs later on.

Myron McDonald, New York expert on television presentations, who has handled numerous political and commercial programs, strongly advises against lengthy television programs as well as "wrap-ups" or telethons at the campaign's close. He recommends television spots of one minute, twenty seconds and eight seconds. The latter sounds almost subliminal but he has much faith in the flash effect. What is needed is not "a juggernaut of propaganda, but a steady rainfall of communication that (will) penetrate and not confront anybody all at once." He recommends that campaign spots be amusing as well as informative and his agency skillfully uses spots with humorous surprise twists at the signoff. As he notes, "You have to give

71

them (the viewers) some little reward in return for their attention." [2]

The effect of television spots wears off quickly and except for essential plugs to make a critical point (such as how to split a ticket or emphasis on an opponent's blunders) should be changed for new visual appeals.

The ideal time for television, obviously, is in the high viewing, high rating night hours, when nearly everybody's home. You will gain maximum coverage if you have the funds to slip in briefly (so as not to annoy the viewer) between two popular network productions. The cost may seem prohibitively high per minute or less, but may be a better buy per person reached than on a daytime show or during the weekend. You may reach about a third of the women during their daytime working hours but you reach very few men until the evening shows come on. Sometimes it is useful to build an audience for longer TV programs by small "teaser" type ads on the TV-radio pages of the local newspapers.

Debates between candidates on television are helpful to voters —and dangerous to candidates—in direct ratio to the lack of insulation of the candidates from the viewer. That is to say, the more direct the confrontation between antagonists, the easier they can get at each other in thrust and parry, the more exciting and the more revealing the effect. From the public's standpoint, the mediator should be no more than referee or occasional goad. TV producers, commentators and contestants generally prefer a panel form of debate where each candidate has a fixed time for presentation of his views and a fixed time to submit to questions from a panel of reporters or from the audience. Of course, where one candidate feels sure that he can take the other's measure, he argues for more direct face-

[2] Myron McDonald, "The Magic of Hard-hitting Political Television Spots," *The Art of Winning Elections,* pp. 88-91.

to-face debate. This is true also where the candidate feels he is running behind and has nothing to lose or where the candidate must get the exposure to even up matters with a better known incumbent.

Preparation before debate is supremely important. Adequate rest beforehand is crucial. It is easy to forget that TV viewers can examine every "wrong line" in a debater's face. Even makeup (once scorned as 'sissified') is usually accepted as essential, varying with color or black and white television. Former Vice President Nixon still refers ruefully to his makeup job on that first historical debate with then Senator John F. Kennedy.

Under the Federal Communications Commission's so-called "Fairness Doctrine," a radio or TV station carrying a discussion of controversial issues of public concern must afford a reasonable opportunity for the broadcast of opposing views. This policy has also been accepted by stations editorializing on a given topic which involves agreement or disagreement with an incumbent or candidate on the subject matter of the editorial. Of course, there must be a clear relationship between the views or actions of the person affected and the content of the editorial.

The "Equal Time" provision requires stations to provide equal opportunity (time and exposure) to all candidates for a public office where time has been extended to any candidate for that office. Keep your eye on pending proposals to grant more free time to major candidates as well as campaign financing reforms in this area.

In using the mass media, concentrate on only one idea at a time. Don't throw in a catch-all of ideas or try to call the roll of issues. You divert attention. If you're selling peaches, there's no reason to put any pears in the package.

Most of the political cognoscenti advise against publicizing your opponent. In one national campaign a presidential candidate never mentioned the incumbent by name (the incumbent won). I recommend that you play this by instinct, yours and your advisers. If your opponent is a shining target you may benefit from highlighting his failures, bumbles or disreputable associates. There is also the fact that if he is the incumbent, he is already better known than you are. If he fires back, your name gets into print again and your contest may move nearer the front pages. I think campaigning against an anonymous opponent has many disadvantages, including the danger of slipping into the rut of generalizations. Names, not ideas, make news. Names, plus good ideas can make better news, if intelligently handled.

Speaking of news, you won't generate much interest, no matter how good your ideas are, unless you can peg your statements to current news events or recent news happenings or unless your *actions*, coupled with your comments, in themselves make news.

Simply to favor improved traffic safety is hardly newsworthy. But to tie it to a bad accident at a hazardous intersection may make an item. Better still, visit the intersection (hopefully with reporters and photographers) and, on the spot, make specific recommendations to relieve the hazard. There may be news also in interviewing neighbors and soliciting their recommendations for safer streets. You are helped more by indignant voters pouring out their grievances to you than by your unsupported wrath as candidate.

Be sure, as the campaign proceeds, that you and your public relations aide brief the press, radio and TV reporters frequently. Be sure you and the reporters understand the ground rules before each meeting starts. Be candid for background information. Take care to have it well understood at all news conferences whether it is (1) a "backgrounder" from which nothing can be quoted, or (2) "for attribution", which means that you are not to be quoted directly but reporters may say "sources close to (the candidate) report" or (3) "it is believed" or the candidate "reportedly feels," etc. Finally, (4) "on the record" news conferences mean just that: no quotes barred. If you say it, you'll have to live with it.

Sometimes a statement in your press release is taken out of context by newspapers or radio or TV reporters. Be very careful that two or three sentences, if pulled out and used alone, are not going to give an entirely different impression than the whole statement intends. Watch your complete statement not only for what it says but for the way the wire services or the radio may edit it. If you do not word your statements with some forethought, you will spend your time saying that what you read is not what you said and trying to retrieve your words —which is the first chapter of "How to get out of politics."

It is a mistake to send too much press material to the small radio station where one or two men do all the engineering, production and newscasting. They simply haven't time to plow through long statements or involved position papers, so most of it dies at the bottom of the pile. Far better to send them a one sentence punch line with your name tied in to a breaking news story. Less work for all hands and better odds on your effort.

Never overlook an opportunity to visit with editors. This gives you a chance for some handshaking in composing rooms as well. Lots of people visit a newspaper office, especially the smaller ones, and your visit will stir up some conversation.

I think an excellent device for a candidate is the one inch ad, interspersed throughout the paper, each pushing a single thought. For example: "Ask his neighbors about Joe Smith, legislative candidate. They like him." Or "Joe Smith, 5th district legislative candidate, has worked 10 years with your youth camps."

Newsletters are often helpful issued periodically to as large a mailing list as you can afford. In your newsletters and brochures you can build up a mailing list by accumulating membership lists of organizations from friends, from programs of meetings, from all sorts of industrial, political and social compilations. You can glean some good names from the daily papers. Use plenty of pictures. Feature endorsements of your candidacy by prominent personalities and well-known organizations. Be cheerful and affirmative. Don't batter your incumbent very much, if at all, in newsletters. This and other campaign literature, if you must be critical, can be usefully enclosed in person-to-person mail.

If you are an incumbent, the robo-typed letter can be quite helpful. Such a letter enables you to direct a special message to a pre-selected group, whereas a newsletter discussion of current issues is shot gun stuff in its general aim and may involve you in needless controversy with one group while helping you with another.

Set up as many committees as you can, of grocers, barbers, lawyers, doctors, ethnic groups and so on. But get more than a "one-shot" story out of the announcement. Give your committees something to do. Have the grocers get some interviews with customers on the cost of living and whodunit. Have the architects inspect, examine and report on housing, parks and traffic problems. Ask a prominent and well-liked person to head up each group. Your campaign volunteers should handle the mailing and between your staff and the committees you will have to find the money for the postage. Get grocers to write to grocers, for example, brief letters stressing but a single argument for you: "I'm sure Joe Smith will do what he can to keep the cost of living down. He's my customer. I trust him. So can you."

I have said little about campaign brochures, buttons, matches, banners, bumper stickers, balloons, billboards, posters, sashes for the "Janes for Joe Smith" girls. You will have fun deciding on more than you can afford, and less fun squirming over what your budget compels you to omit. Here again, the objective advice of a professional in public relations is preferable to the arguments of salesmen of campaign gimmicks. For a personal campaign memory jogger, I prefer to hand out pens or pencils with my name and office imprinted. You will probably be more pleased with rulers, calendars or combs or whatnot. One Congressional candidate rode to success on potholders personally handed to housewives at their doors. My Pennsylvania wife got hold of one and used that Connecticut potholder for six years.

Early endorsements, well publicized, from prominent people, will help to get you better known. Further endorsements at the very end can help put your effort across the line. It's a tenstrike for you if you can persuade former primary opponents or those who were once adverse to you, to come across with an endorsement. More effective still are endorsements from persons in the opposing political party. You may find that photographs with the President, former presidents, governors and others will aid in your publicity. Even more helpful may be speeches for you or visits to your district by well-known (if well-liked!) public officials.

Here two warning markers bob in your path. One, your opponent may attack your visitors as meddlers or "carpetbaggers" and voters may prefer to make their choice without outside advice. Two, you may be utterly overshadowed by your distinguished visitors and suffer from comparisons meeting the public's eye. Once, in a major city, the favored candidate for Mayor suffered politically because of the wide disparity between his modest attributes and the glamorous presence of the Vice President and a well-known Senator who praised him beyond the area of public credibility. Between the upper and the nether millstones of their prestige, they managed to grind him too finely.

There are many ways to sell the contagion of a campaign. What you are aiming for is the physical evidence of great and growing enthusiasm. Surround yourself with young people—in the headquarters, at meetings, street rallies, all along the campaign trail. They make more noise—and happier sounds. I mentioned "Janes for Joe." Have pretty young girls with campaign sashes, colorful hats and dresses to glamor up the activities and catch the eye of audiences and press and TV cameramen. To the Fourth Estate, politicians are old hat, but there's still nothing like a dame.

A catchy, constantly blazoned and repeated campaign slogan is a good idea. I've used such slogans as "Hugh's For *You*," "Great Scott" and "Experience Counts." Stress what you think is your strongest quick selling point.

Much employed are campaign sound trucks with recorded speakers or music. Keep them out of quiet neighborhoods, especially during the babies' nap time. And keep the volume down below a roar. There are campaigners who don't believe noise sells at all. It's a matter of judgment and what your constituency is used to.

If there is a lot of geography to cover in your district, a campaign bus can be employed. They are for hire, outfitted for work, storage of campaign material and even room for a snooze on the road and a refrigerated snack bar.

A good way to help voters remember you is to employ your own photographer to go where you go. He should try for unusual pictures, which have a better chance of landing in the local press coverage. As an example of offbeat camera work, my photographer, avoiding pictures of baby kissing politicians, snapped an unforgettable picture of a five year old blonde kissing a huge blowup of the candidate. A good photographer can also catch you taking part in active sports or at offbeat hours such as dawn factory tours or nighttime county fairs when regular press cameramen are not available.

My able public relations adviser, Gene Cowen, who has run many successful campaigns for candidates, originated the now often used instant camera technique. The candidate or one of his staff photograph constituents and give them the autographed picture on the spot. Such pictures are likely to be shown around and are working for you everytime they are pulled out of someone's pocket.

Finally, plan your campaign with utmost care, gear it to your budget, adhere closely to your schedule, don't miss meetings and be on time, if humanly possible. This advice might seem to have been better included under the chapter on campaigning, but it's here because excellence in planning and competence in execution are good public relations.

The press condemn nepotism, that is putting *private* relations on your payroll. But your success may depend on your making full provision for *public* relations there.

8. Running to Win

WOULD you like to run for office? If so, as Grover Cleveland said, in another context, "The way to begin is to begin." My best advice is to begin by making sure you want to enter upon a lifetime of political activity. Among the disadvantages—or advantages—to the political person is that as surely as you run for office, especially if at first you win, you're hooked. "Few die and none resign" goes the old saw. While some give the political wheel a brief, experimental spin, returning to more quiet ways, there is something greatly infectious about this merry-go-round. To decide when to get off the carrousel and pick up a new life is not always simple. The exits are not clearly marked.

You will find the life exciting if you like people, lots of them, and if you thrive on excitement and cliff-hanging uncertainties. There is the other side of it: the disruption of family life, the unexpected expenditures, the disappointments and the difficulty of picking up another career if you've tarried too long at the political fair—all these are hostages you must render to fortune. By far the most common regret among legislators is this: "I have seen too little of my family; I wish I had seen more of my children as they were growing up."

Having been duly warned, the next step, if you savor the thought of political candidacy, is to determine your objective, whether it be executive or legislative office. Whatever your ultimate target, you will rarely, as I have noted elsewhere, begin at the top. Assuming that you have already been active in political work in some aspect, you will have discovered the kind of political office to which you aspire.

So scout around and decide what office you would like to run for. This will be governed by what's open. Some offices may be firmly held by popular incumbents, others may be electorally closed for the time being to your political party because of the massive power of the other party. Even here, however, there have been a number of instances of surprising upsets achieved by exceptionally hard working candidates.

To establish a frame of reference, let us suppose that you decide to become a candidate for the state legislature if you can garner support sufficient to warrant the try.

If you can garner support—that's the first key to unlock a series of doors. Learn the voting history and voting habits of your legislative district. Appraise the situation and evaluate your chances: Who are the other likely candidates? What is the nature of their backing? Who will have the most to say in the approval of a candidate in the primary election?

You can make your own survey of sorts. Discuss your ambitions and your prospects with your friends, especially the politically acute ones. Of most importance, perhaps, is to talk to those who mold opinion in your community. Opinion makers include business, farm and labor leaders, publishers, editors, TV and radio owners, reporters, commentators, clergymen, educators. The decision makers will very probably be political leaders who are normally open to persuasion by public opinion, which in turn is greatly influenced by the opinion makers. Public relations experts advise generally: get your gentle persuasion working very early and work on your voters over a long period of time.

You may also make your contribution to public opinion by sending up trial balloons. These consist of statements by you indicative of your interest in the post and by speculative items filtering through the press, radio or TV. Reaction to this toe-dipping may help you to reach your decision.

It may be that you will not be the choice of political leaders. They may recommend another to the party unit or direct to the public. At this point you will have to decide whether to fight it out at the primary election against one or more other candidate or whether to abide the adverse decision, pick up points for future use for being a good sport and to work to improve your chances when the next opportunity opens up.

The announcement of your candidacy should be timed, if you can manage it, to secure maximum publicity. Consulting with experienced politicians or a public relations expert can be helpful both as to the time and method you adopt to break the news —or to break into it.

Now that you are committed to your campaign, your success depends upon your campaign resources: people, issues, information, publicity, and, essential to mobilizing all your assets, an effective campaign organization.

Choose your campaign manager carefully. You are looking for loyalty, competence, organizing ability, energy and the ability to get along with people. If your man is high in all these qualities you are well set for your takeoff.

Next persuade a persuasive friend to be the chairman of your fund raising committee. The best ideas won't help you much unless you can project them through campaign material and via the media of communications. All that takes money. You need a patient, persistent and experienced separater of funds from people, helped by a zealous committee.

I strongly advise retention of competent public relations assistance as the first paid associate—even if he turns out to be the only one.

You will find many uses for volunteers but don't put your fate in the hands of a volunteer public relations type.

A good candidate deserves and needs good organization, good financing and some professionalism in those areas where objectivity added to experience can make the difference. Be sure to ring your own key workers into your inner strategy. Use plenty of helmsmen but only one compass.

Before launching your active campaign, get the facts about our potential constituency. William S. Roberts of Spencer-Roberts & Associates, California specialists in campaign management, makes a good point:

"You sit down at a meeting with a half dozen people, and they state, 'yes, we've got quite a few ethnic people living over here at this end of the district.'

"I say, 'How many?'

" 'Well, I don't know. Quite a few. Several precincts.'

"I want to know exactly how many. I want to know how old they are. I want to know what their economic status is. I want to know what their educational status is. I want to know what they've done in previous elections, given a particular set of circumstances. I want to know everything about those people that I possibly can. This information helps make for successful races."

He adds: "Many campaigns are not won by what you do but what mistakes you don't make." [1]

There are many ways to go about getting the facts to guide your strategy. These include: the use of surveys and polls, marketing surveys, data compiled by political, labor, farm or business organizations, through the use of directory services, and from informants experienced in the makeup and problems of the district.

John Deardourff, former Research Director of the New York Republican State Campaign, gives good counsel on the importance of careful research. He states: ". . . good research can intensify public concern about problems. It can raise the level of awareness of the public about community problems; it

---

[1] William E. Roberts, "Public Relations—Keystone To Victory," *The Art of Winning Elections* (Washington, D. C.: Republican National Committee, 1967), p. 54.

can create an atmosphere of greater interest and greater receptivity to the campaign and to your candidate." [2]

Deardourff suggests six general areas of campaign research:

1. Research on the ward, city, district, county or state itself.

2. Research on past voting trends, of your own past record and anything relevant to party positions. Also track down the history of ticket splitting and percentage of switchable voters.

3. Public opinion research or polling. "Polling is only valuable if it's done well, if it's done professionally . . ." to provide "you with good, solid professional information. A bad poll is worse than no poll at all. . . ." A good poll should ". . . tell you how the public is likely to respond to given positions which you may take."

4. The research on your opponent, both as to past record and present positions, should help you to generate questions which can force your adversary to commit himself on matters he doesn't want to discuss.

5. Research on major issues in the campaign. Don't waste time on too many minor issues.

6. Local interest or special interest research is advisable. These may not be important throughout your area or throughout the campaign but may be immensely important locally. Consider the advisability of storefront headquarters. They may help the main research headquarters with useful local feedback as to what problems are stirring up a neighborhood.[3]

Plan carefully the timing of your campaign. Decide where and when to establish issues and discuss them, prepare your

---

[2] John Deardourff, "How To Utilize Research Data In Developing A Campaign Program," *Republican Victories Through Public Relations* (Washington, D. C.: Republican National Committee, 1966), Section VI, pp. 1-2.

[3] *Ibid.*, pp. 2-10.

campaign budget, lay out the timing of your television and radio campaigns for maximum effect, organize your volunteers and your 'people to people' program and remember, it's important to start early but even more important to finish fast.

I am indebted to L. Richard Guylay, publicist, for an excellent summation of the ingredients for success in campaigning. He identifies the basic persuaders as "prestige, affirmation, repetition and contagion."

By prestige he simply means get a good candidate, an achiever, preferably a natural leader. If this is no Cinderella slipper problem for you, let's go on to "affirmation".

Affirmation requires concise statement of your case in sharp, simple, readily understandable terms. He quotes Gustav LeBon: "Affirmation . . . has no significance unless it is constantly repeated, and so far as possible in the same terms."

Repetition. The necessity for this is obvious. Bear in mind what I have said about speechmaking. Tell your audience what you are going to tell them. Then tell them. And then tell them what you have told them. Continue to tell your story as often and in as many places and with as much publicity as possible.

In campaigning work starts early and contagion comes late, if at all. Plan then for a strong finish. Come on strong in the last few weeks. Plan for a buildup of momentum. Contagion is sparked by *sound* (songs, rallies, P.A. systems, TV and radio commercials) and by *sight*. As Guylay says: "You want the sight of contagion, crowds of happy people fighting to shake your . . . hands . . . filling banquet halls with big crowds, and staffing headquarters."

You can sell contagion too by spreading around the campaign paraphernalia of buttons, banners, balloons, posters, billboards, sound trucks, skywriting, anything which colorfully plugs your candidacy.[4]

---

[4] L. Richard Guylay, "How To Develop A Public Relations Program" *The Art of Winning Elections,* pp. 121-125.

In all of this, except where circumstances dictate otherwise, the candidate's organization (while it tries to reach all voters) concentrates its hardest efforts on the non-members of his party, so long as the candidate is satisfied that his party organization is doing the work expected of it in getting out the party vote.

Go where the votes are. This does not mean that you neglect to work on the uncommitted. Far from it. But there will be areas in your constituency where the population is more dense (no offense intended!) than in other areas sparsely settled. To illustrate, in New York State, fifteen of its 62 counties account for eighty percent of the vote. In Pennsylvania, nineteen of its 67 counties contain over seventy-five percent of the total vote. The same is true of legislative districts outside of central urban areas.

Work especially on the "swing" vote. Check vote analyses of previous elections to ascertain where voters switched readily among candidates and between parties and find out why.

Having learned the nature of your district and its problems, develop your issues carefully so that when you go to the people your presentations will be lucid and rememberable.

Another public relations expert, David Brunell of Michigan, suggests certain ground rules: Avoid excessive partisanship. Voters want their candidates to be more than hatchet men. Yet let the issues be direct, challenging and controversial.[5]

Talk in down to earth terms. Identify with the problems of the average man and woman. Involve yourself by on-the-spot inspection of troublesome conditions. Stay with the issues. Don't wander into extraneous or vague areas. *You* pick the issues, Brunell exhorts. Don't let your opponent do it. Find some catchy phrases or slogans to highlight issues and remember the value of repetition. Once more, don't pretend to have *all* the answers and don't be afraid to admit mistakes. Candor

[5] See David Brunell, "How To Unseat A Democratic Congressman," *The Art of Winning Elections,* pp. 160-177.

muffles controversy and enhances your chance of walking away from a "boner" with as few scars as possible.

Your campaign will attract more favorable attention if you come up with new ideas, new directions, initiatives and alternatives that will appeal and attract. In other words: think.

To get time for thinking you will do well to pace yourself. Provide for, and insist upon, intervals to think and to rest up. Don't overheat your motor. These time outs are always helpful in the long run, and especially so before debates, confrontations with your opponent and major speeches. A tired candidate is worse than no candidate.

Since you are not the incumbent, you may need to establish first of all the case for change of personalities, attitudes and programs. It is a good idea to get these negative issues out of the way in the first part of your campaign. This may occur during the period when voters are still registering, and, if so, you may have a chance to influence their choice of party designations.

After disposing of the negative, accentuate the positive. As the old song goes: "Don't mess with Mr. Inbetween." Come on strong with positive approaches, hit them hard and emphasize in your speeches that you are being constructive through affirmative proposals.

The role of a candidate's wife must never be underestimated. Not only will you welcome the day-to-day assurance but you will benefit from her advice and even more from her candid observations. Don't be too quick, or too sensitive, to react to her suggestions as criticisms. Hold still and remember she's on your side. Many candidates' wives make highly effective speeches. Others help by attending meetings with you or by representing you when you must be elsewhere. Some wives garner more intelligence than the FBI could get for you. Read over your speeches to your wife before delivery. She can detect, more readily than subjective you, the unintended note of pomposity or arrogance. She may also react strongly against some idea or favorite scheme. Better listen to her. Other women may well feel the same way.

A few closing thoughts: Avoid defensive positions. Don't campaign from weakness. Don't rely on tricks, evasiveness or sabotage.

Remember when to do nothing. Some attacks had better go unanswered. Dance to your own music. Don't be panicked into hasty reaction. Tomorrow's crisis quickly displaces today's panic. Memory is fleeting. It's not as important to thousands of others as it seems to you. Look around the house. Where is day-before-yesterday's newspaper?

Why do people vote for a candidate? I'll tell you very simply. By far the most compelling reason is because somebody asked them to. As I've noted elsewhere, people love to be asked for their vote. It's a favor—inexpensive to them—which they can confer, but unasked, uncast, could be costly to you.

Therefore, make maximum use of volunteers and assign them vote soliciting, person to person jobs by direct contact, telephone and letter.

Have a committee to help voters secure and send in absentee ballots. This has been so useful in some elections as to make the difference. I recall one election where I trailed by 142,000 votes in my big city (although I won the election). Yet our absentee ballot committee worked so effectively as to bring in nearly the same number of absentee ballots as did my opponent. And I carried three counties by the margin of the absentee ballot lead.

Your friends who do not live in your district can help you too. Ask them to get out their Christmas lists and write a good word for you to their friends who do live in your district.

Be sure to say "thanks" to your supporters *before* Election Day. One good way is by a newspaper ad. So doing, you please them and spur them on to one last burst of activity. You could couple this with a bi-partisan appeal to all eligible citizens to do their civic duty. Thus you close your campaign on a high note.

Choose your headquarters with an eye to central location, ease of access, visibility and attractiveness. You may decide to have more than one headquarters. The use of neighborhood storefronts or of residences of workers can be considered. But avoid dilapidated buildings or empty locations with nothing but a few forlorn banners.

The staging or encouragement of mock elections in high schools or colleges is desirable on one condition: Do you think the result will be favorable?

On Election Day you will, of course, be visiting the polls and receiving progress reports. On Election Night, what happens at your headquarters will depend on whether or not your sterling qualities have been electorally approved by the voters' stamp.

Whether it's victory, or the Other Thing, remember that Kipling may have been corny but he was right in advising that both victory or defeat must be treated just the same—in other words with good sportsmanship. If you've won, be generous to your opponent. He's lost; he wanted the job too. Be kind to him—he's feeling pretty badly.

This is meant to be a cheerful book, so we'll assume you have been elected and that you intend to be a credit to your constituents. Do I have any further advice for you? Not really. Except that a lot of first class officeholders have begun to campaign intelligently the day after Election Day for their re-election.

9. "Ladies and Gentlemen—"

You can buy lots of good books on Public Speaking—the Art of. This does not assume to be one of them. If you wish to know how to tuck in your diaphragm or whatever it is you should do with it during oratorical effort, there are teachers of public speaking in the nearest city or town. There you may be instructed in matters such as breath control, enunciation, posture, timing, and many technical ins and outs that should be most helpful. This chapter's purpose is but to discuss some possibly useful hints on making a speech or conducting a public meeting.

Not all public speakers will agree with everything set down here; for instance, little will be offered on how to be a great orator. The emphasis will be on presentation of your ideas to a group of people in acceptable and possibly persuasive form.

I have been standing on public platforms for more than forty years; I have spoken in public thousands of times. I am still nervous before nearly every speech, and I never have the slightest idea how it will turn out—whether it will prove to be above or below the standards I have set for myself. As to whether the audience likes it or not, one can never really be sure about that. People are usually polite in their remarks to the speaker afterward. But you get a feeling about those things. You are apt to say to yourself, "That was not as good as I should have liked it to be," or "Everything went all right tonight but I should have stopped five minutes sooner." (You probably should have stopped ten minutes sooner.)

Bryce Harlow, speechwriter for President Eisenhower and other V.I.P.'s, warns against boredom in a too-long speech, the "buzz signal," when the audience starts visiting instead of listening. He likewise opts for precision as far outweighing rhetoric, and lucidity rather than that cleverness which diverts attention from thoughts to words.[1]

Are you a natural public speaker? I doubt it. It is questionable whether there is such a thing as a natural public speaker except in the sense that one may be called a natural pianist. The finished product in either case results only from a considerable amount of practice. Burnishing comes after a good deal of study and experience. I am aware that I have said elsewhere in this book that any person who can talk can talk in public. But the more practice you have, the more facility; the more experience you gain, the more confidence you will have. "Skill in speaking is perfected by nature, art and practice."—Quintilian.

You may have a very real gift for public speaking without being at all aware of it until an occasion arises when you feel the urge to express yourself on a matter in which you are much interested. You are anxious to discuss it before others whom you would like to persuade to your way of thinking. When that occurs you may be surprised to find that you are speaking with more ease of expression than you thought you had.

You will not be the first speaker to discover this. A United States Senator and former university president writes of his first essay at public speaking:

> After three months of personal visits, with particular attention to those persons known to be influential in political matters, the speaking campaign began. This phase of the campaign is downright hard work. Never having made a political speech, the first few efforts were excruciatingly painful. I have seldom experienced a feeling of more abject despair and humiliation than the first time I spoke on the street corner of a small village with about a dozen curious listeners who apparently were not listening. However, it is amazing how soon

[1] Bryce Harlow, "How To Write An Effective Political Speech," *Republican Victories Through Public Relations,* Section IX.

one becomes accustomed to the sound of one's voice when forced to repeat a speech five or six times a day. As election day approaches, the size of the crowds grows; they are more responsive and more interested, and one derives a certain exhilaration from that which, a few weeks before was intensely painful.*

Suppose we break up our discussion about your speech into (a) your theme, (b) its preparation, and (c) its delivery.

In selecting your theme, be sure it is of current interest and that you are talking about something you know more about than your audience. At the very least, be sure that you understand enough about the subject so that you are not in danger of getting in beyond your depth. Hang your knapsack where you can reach it. Your subject should be of current interest; this is most important. You may be quite an expert on the coinage of ancient Rome or Audubon prints but a political audience will not be composed entirely of numismatists or bird lovers.

It is desirable to select but a single main topic for your subject matter. You do not want to overburden your audience as you skip from local to national issues, from the state budget to the missing manhole covers on Main Street. You want them to remember what you have said. Your chances are better if you remember that they hope to enjoy themselves or at the least to receive your speech as painlessly as possible; they cannot be expected to assimilate a junior encyclopedia in one sitting. It is more to the point that your hearers should recall one telling argument than that they should be impressed, while you have them at your mercy, with the wide range of your interests. The purpose of speaking is to communicate ideas. One idea at a time is a good average.

---

* Hon. J. William Fulbright, U.S. Senator from Arkansas, *Think,* publication of International Business Machine Corporation, New York, Aug. 1946.

If in the development of your thought it is necessary to consider several subdivisions of your main theme, it will contribute to clarity if you summarize these in 1-2-3 or a-b-c fashion, both at the beginning and at the end of your talk. This has the added virtue of keeping your audience posted as to how nearly through you are; it gives them strength to stick with you, to maintain their concentration a while longer. Without the help of some such signposts along your oratorical way, your audience has no idea how long you may ramble on, and they may, mentally, go away from there.

Tailor your theme to your audience. Audiences are people, and people are primarily concerned with their own interests. Therefore, you are aiming at a known target; your appeal must be made directly to personal interest. Know your audience. Learn something of their background and their interests. Apt use of local references will help you establish a rapport with your listeners. Like the Bailey bridges laid by Army engineers under fire in order to get across a stream in a hurry, you must quickly build a bridge in full sight of your audience in order to span the gap between your as-yet-undelivered views and their interest in what you may have to say. You get across that bridge by impressing upon your listeners that it will be to their personal advantage to know more about what you are going to tell them.

Bacon says, "The proofs and demonstrations of logic are toward all men indifferent and the same, but the proofs and persuasions of rhetoric ought to differ according to the auditors." Give careful thought to the make-up of your audience so that you may shape the content of your remarks within the scope of their interests and experience. Don't be patronizing. Don't stoop to conquer. It is essential not to talk above or below your audience; either way they will resent it. So a little thought about this may save your speech for you. To be interesting, and through interest to persuade, bring your ideas within the vivid experience of your listeners.

Assuming that the main purpose in the development of your theme will be to persuade your audience to accept your premises and conclusions, what props will you use to support your presentation? You may select an informative or narrative approach or you may decide that a vigorous attack will prove most effective; perhaps you may achieve the best results by a combination of these. And how and to what extent will you make use of humor, eulogy, or inspirational material?

Usually a speech seeking immediate, overt action will contain a greater proportion of emotional appeal than one which seeks "delayed action," and the latter will often contain more logical material than the former, but this statement is subject to many exceptions. In very few cases should the speaker omit either logical argument or motive-appeal. . . . And Overstreet in *Influencing Human Behavior,* puts the idea in vivid form when he says, "No appeal to reason that is not at the same time an appeal to wants can ever succeed."
—*Principles of Effective Speaking*—Sandford and Yeager.

Another suggestion by the same authorities will be helpful.

1. The main ideas should be the *reasons for accepting* the belief or acting on the issue.
2. The main ideas should be *appeals to motives* for action.
3. The main ideas should be chosen in such a way as to overcome objections.*

I might add, the main idea is to get them to vote for you or your candidate.

After selection of the theme of a speech and planning its development come the considerations governing its preparation.

How will you put your speech together?

Having selected a topic and considered its skeletal outlines, commit your thoughts to paper. As you write out your draft, be

---

* Ibid.

guided by one of the safest rules in the business: begin by telling your audience what you are going to tell; then tell it, and conclude by telling your audience what you have told.

It is well to have your speech written out in full unless you are a very accomplished professional. Whether you plan to read your speech (of which more later when we come to discuss its delivery) or whether you plan to speak from notes, the possession of the written speech will give you a better grasp of your subject, and it will give you confidence to know that you have it if you need it. Furthermore, if you do speak from notes, your memory will be aided by having committed the entire effort to writing. A written speech avoids misquotation or, if deliberately distorted later by your opposition, furnishes you with effective refutation. Also, the written speech will be useful, in whole or in part, for advance press releases or to hand to reporters at the meeting. Do not read your speech if you can muster the confidence to deliver it orally.

You may have been told how much time your speech should take. In the case of radio or TV speeches you will always know this—even to the seconds. If you must decide for yourself, decide in favor of brevity. Audience attention is very uncertain after twenty minutes and that is stretching it a bit. Some clergymen say that "no souls are saved after the first fifteen minutes." And in the last ten minutes you can lose friends you have made in the first twenty. It may hurt a little for you to cut out your own words after you have put them down with some effort, but if it seems ruthless at the time, be assured that the end result is nearly always an improvement. Your thoughts will have been expressed more compactly, the less fat the more meat.

Aristotle refers to the four points of a speech as: exordium, statement, proof, epilogue. In your exordium or introductory remarks you have your chance to warm up your audience. They must be won by your opening sentences. An arresting opening sentence, followed by one even more arresting, is a most important opening gambit. You must establish a personal intimacy between yourself and your audience. Local allusions to matters of interest to your listeners in their own community and complimentary references to local personages or to other participants in the meeting can play their part in establishing this intimacy.

Anecdotes or humorous stories, especially if they lead naturally into your subject matter, can often be used to advantage, especially in the early part of your speech while your audience is settling down and getting ready to give its attention to what you have to say. It is for good reason that the first few minutes of the first act of a play are fairly inconsequential; it takes a while for attention to come to a focus on the play itself.

The purpose of your introductory remarks, then, is to get attention. But come to the point. Be as brief in your opening as you can. Get attention, get it quickly, and move on to the body of your speech—to your statement and your proof, *i.e.,* to the reasons for accepting your belief or acting on them and to the appeal to motives for action.

In constructing the body of your speech, be logical, be fair, be aggressive if the situation calls for it, but do not lose sight of your motive: to persuade. Persuasion may be achieved most readily through temperate use of language, through your earnestness in presentation, and through sagacious blending of reason and emotion to convince the listeners that their interests will be served by acceptance of the position you are advancing.

Determine where you are going to lay your basic emphasis, to whom you are planning to appeal and with what arguments. Set up the subdivisions of your main theme, inlay them briefly and clearly, intersperse with allusions and comparisons that will be within the experience of your audience to comprehend, and stay away as much as possible from musty statistics and from abstractions generally. Talk about problems as they affect human beings or about live, current issues, but keep away from tiresome generalizations and philosophizing. Put in some new ideas.

To know how to end a speech is as important as to know how to brake a car. No matter how winning may be your speech up to now, you can ruin it all if you drag wearily to an inconclusive close because of your lack of terminal facilities. You must avoid anticlimax.

A conclusion may end with a summation of the points you have made, or it may end by a call for a decision or action, motivated by the logic and the emotional appeal of your discourse. Or it may be a combination of both, in which case the summation should come first. You will want to end on a high note and to sit down while the audience is still willing to hear more.

Now that your speech is written what happens to it next depends upon your delivery. The effective communication of your ideas depends upon the quality of your delivery, in other words the way you put your ideas across to your audience. "The orator must instruct, move and please his hearers," says our old friend, that informative Roman, Quintilian. The instruction lies both in the content and the way in which it is presented, but whether you are to move your auditors to belief or action and whether you are to please them depends most of all upon the way in which you communicate your ideas to those who are present to receive them.

If, through familiarity with your subject, you are sure of what you are going to say and the order in which you are going to proceed from one idea to another, you will have freed your mind to permit you to consider the most effective way of communicating those ideas as you go along.

The secret of good delivery is naturalness and sincerity. Look upon your audience as friends and neighbors with whom you are exchanging mutually interesting ideas. If they feel that you are warmly disposed to them, they will warm up to you. As you speak more and more often, you will find that you tend to develop a personal style best suited to your temperament, but beware of eccentricities—they will only distract your audience and detract from your delivery.

Do not include material in your speech that you cannot deliver with conviction, because your sincerity and earnestness of voice and manner must spring from your belief in the ideas you are advancing. To carry conviction to others, you must have it yourself. It is essential for the speaker to convey to the audience by manner, gestures and tone that he is in deadly earnest (without being deadly dull) and that he has something of the utmost importance and interest to convey to them.

If your whole manner is alive and alert, if it is obvious that you are under control but, feeling the inner tension of your deeply held convictions, you will keep your audience on its toes. They will react to the mood you set if you throw yourself wholeheartedly into the communication of that feeling. Grow soporific in delivery and your listeners will accommodate you with restless shufflings, yawns and coughings.

There are times when a speech must be read with close adherence to the written text; there are other meetings where it is far better not to read a speech but to speak from memory or from an outline. A full-dress speech on an important occasion may be read because of the danger of misunderstanding or the undesirable consequences that might follow from inadequately considered ad-lib remarks. This is especially so when an important speech is being covered by the press. Speeches on technical subjects or scholarly theses are also usually read, but these will not often be presented upon political occasions. If you must read your speech, do so slowly, being careful to place proper emphasis on your main ideas.

On reading speeches, a story is told of a young Scottish dominie, delivering his first sermon at his new kirk. After the sermon, he pressed his oldest and most important parishioner for a candid opinion. The old hardshell replied, "Aweel, since ye insist, I'll gie ye ma answer: I didna' like it: in the fur-rst place, ye read it; in the second place, ye read it bodly; in the thur-rd place, it wasn'a wur-th the readin'."

Generally speaking, you should memorize your speech or talk from an outline. Speakers who follow an outline know when they're through. Be sure you know when you're through and so indicate near the end of your talk, before your audience starts praying for such an assurance. Many speakers write out their entire speech (others write out a rough draft), then prepare notes on a card, small sheet of paper or back of an envelope. These notes may consist of the principal points you are going to make with allusions or anecdotes noted in abbreviated form, or they may consist of the opening lines of each paragraph. You will learn through experience whether you prefer to use this or some other shorthand method of memory jogger. Your ability to commit your whole speech to memory may be such that you will not need notes. (But you will need to avoid sounding like a mechanical man.) If you have that good a memory, there are many who will envy you, including myself.

A sense of timing will grow on you; pauses at the proper places are useful, not only for emphasis but because a pause attracts the audience's attention to the idea you wish to get across. A pause after you make your point crystallizes the idea in the mind of your listeners.

Stick to the subject. Don't wander verbosely all over the lot. Beware of wool gathering. Do not be tempted by a random word or sudden flash of inspiration during your delivery to explore a lot of side alleys unless you can see pretty clearly what is down there. Don't cover too much territory. Leave that to Rand-McNally.

Tinge what you have to say with good humor and speak with becoming modesty. Too high a markup on your wares may lead your customers to make their own discounts.

HOW TO RUN FOR PUBLIC OFFICE, AND WIN!

When you use anecdotes, use those that have some bearing on your theme or that can be tied in to it. An aimless joke may set your audience to searching for the connection with what you are talking about rather than to continue to listen to what you are saying. Sometimes an apt story will suggest itself to you while you are listening to the speaker who precedes you on the program or while you are going over your speech in your mind as you politely make small talk with your neighbor at the banquet table.

Don't tell jokes unrelated to your speech just to get a laugh—they usually don't, as your presiding officer has already discovered if he has tried the same gambit. This sort of labored funny story doesn't impress the audience and transition to your topic becomes too abrupt.

There are ways to ring the changes on some story you have heard so that it will fit snugly into your opening remarks. Suppose you have heard a story about a man who was entertaining two prominent churchmen at dinner, a Methodist and a Baptist. In the kitchen he prepared their dessert, watermelon, by dousing it liberally with whisky and after having it served sat down to watch the results. The Methodist turned to his slice with joyful appetite, but our friend noticed that the Baptist was busily engaged in covertly stuffing the seeds into his pocket. Well, you don't want to draw comparisons between Methodists and Baptists in a political meeting, but what's to prevent you from substituting Democrats and Republicans?

Many speakers have a tendency to drop their voices at the end of a sentence. In speaking, keep your voice up but watch out—don't get shrill or harsh. It is a good rule to direct your voice to the last row in which people are sitting and keep an eye on them from time to time to see if they appear to be hearing you. If you are in doubt don't be afraid to stop and ask if you are being heard. It is better than for you to be inaudible, and your audience will apprecite your consideration. Variations

100

in volume and pitch of your voice depend upon control of your breathing and of your vocal cords, respectively. Any public-speaking teacher will explain to you, if you wish, how you may perfect your technique in this direction. Above all, don't yell!

Try to make the people you are talking to feel that you are speaking to them individually. Stay away from a monotone and you are less likely to sound as if you were talking to yourself. Listen to yourself: are you uh-ing and ah-ing? Set yourself consciously to get rid of the habit. You can do it, but the chances are that you will have to keep working at it for a while. It is a mannerism that is peculiarly distracting to an audience. The effectiveness gained from its excision is worth the effort.

Remember as you draw to the close of your speech that you are coming to the most important part. Do not mutter wearily or miserably as you turn to your seat, "I thank you"—the world's most insincere ending, by the way—but leave your hearers with something informative, striking, or moving to remember you by. It is what they hear last that they remember the longest.

There are differing points of view as to the political value of forums on public questions. As many candidates see it, there is more to be lost than gained from a live debate between adversaries, especially where the audience participates in a question period. There is certainly a possibility of detriment where one candidate appears and his adversary does not. One would think that this situation would reflect on the absentee, but actually the candidate present is under blankets—he is liable to criticism for attacking one who is not present to reply (even though willfully absent)—and I remember vividly one candidate, an inexperienced and shy speaker, who drew this aside from a lady in the audience, "I don't think much of him; I think I'll vote for the other man"—whom she had never seen!

Even where both candidates appear, there is the possibility that sparks struck on the anvil of debate may lead to some unfortunate outburst that will cause a loss of sympathy for the speaker disproportionate to the merits of his whole case. Or the audience may have been packed to the disadvantage of one side or the other with the result that the questions directed at one of the candidates are heavily loaded. As in the forum at Rome, the audience may enjoy it, but the gladiators murder each other.

Even so, the right of the public to know its candidates, to size them up, to hear both sides, is or should be the paramount consideration. There is a lot to be said in favor of the old South Carolina system where the opposing candidates rode the circuit together, appearing on the same platform before gatherings throughout the state.

There is some doubt as to whether a great many people change their opinions as a result of forum appearances. But after all, whether they do or not, is it not in the public interest that the people should see and hear those who wish to manage the public's business?

If you are participating in a forum or open debate, keep in mind that the best opportunity you will have to make effective arguments will generally come by way of rebuttal to something your adversary has said. In your main talk you sometimes set up paper targets and knock them down as readily as you set them up. In rebuttal, you are in a live bout and every blow counts. So it's up to you to make your maximum effort.

As an example of repartee, consider this incident occurring in the days of the Grecian public assemblies: After a long and brilliant speech promising great happenings, an Athenian, who lacked eloquence but was of known courage, got up and said, "Men of Athens, All that he has said, I will do."

Resort to the radio and television in political campaigning has tended to reduce the number of political meetings and rallies. Many people have learned that they may follow the development of a political controversy with so much less effort by turning a dial or moving a knob. Speaking on TV or radio may vastly increase the number and heterogeneity of your hearers, but the communication of your ideas to them is now accompanied by new limitations. You will have a more difficult time of it in projecting your personality, on which you relied to hold attention when speaking to a live audience. Yet the need to hold attention becomes many times greater. They now can walk out on you without scruple, and you won't even know they are leaving.

Your main idea is still to move your audience to belief or action, but retaining their attention must now also receive high priority as you plan your speech.

Write out your speech in full; have it typed in clear, legible form, double-spaced and not too much on each sheet. Find out exactly how much time you have; a fifteen-minute speech may mean, minus announcements and conclusion, thirteen minutes and fifty seconds; a five-minute talk, four minutes and ten seconds. Then time your speech very carefully. Time it several times at the speed at which you expect to deliver it, then note on the side of your pages the expiration of minutes or half minutes. If you are still short on TV or radio experience, you will probably take just a little longer to deliver it than you think you will. It helps to guard against emergencies by marking certain sentences toward the end that you can leave out if the studio clock tells you that you must. If you find that you are likely to finish ahead of time, the studio is often prepared for that with music or other fillers, but you can usually manage well enough by slowing down, not too perceptibly, or by inserting sentences you may have typed out on an extra page against that eventuality. This latter device is awkward to manage and is not especially recommended. Accurate timing or studio signals are your best bet. Some speakers use teleprompters or "idiot boards", i.e., big signs with principal points written in large letters. Either visual aid will help to maintain eye contact with a TV audience and you won't have to bob your head up and down from your notes.

As to the content of your speech, keep thinking about the universality of your audience. What you say must be of general interest and, as you progress, knowing how quickly they can dial you out and get some good music or a sports event, seek to sustain interest in what you are going to say next. Hold out to these invisible souls that something even more interesting is coming as you proceed; then impress on them by logic, emotion, and the earnestness of your delivery why that which you are telling them is to their advantage, why they should believe or act on what you are advocating. On television, look into the glowing red eye below the camera. It won't hurt to be a little folksy and mention your audience in their living room, but don't be coy! Avoid statistics as much as possible and where you must use them, resort to eye-catching props or charts, to analogy or comparison with down-to-earth day-to-day experiences.

Don't harangue your auditors. And don't yell. On the TV or radio it comes out even worse than on the platform. And never engage more than fifteen minutes of TV or radio time even if you can get it and can afford it. That is long enough— it may even be more than long enough—and your audience is accustomed to short political programs. Fifteen or 30 second spot plugs are even better.

There is room for a great deal of argument as to just how and when TV and radio are effective in political campaigns. Certainly, if used too far in advance of election day, they are not used to the best advantage. Many experienced campaigners think that fifteen-minute political talks are a waste of time except in the case of those who spearhead a campaign, such as candidates for president, governor, or senator, or in those instances where public interest is thoroughly aroused in a hot issue and the speaker is directly involved in, or especially informed about, its development.

Campaign managers have discovered that the number of listeners to political speeches is measurably increased if advance publicity is contracted for in local newspapers. These "tune-in" ads should feature the speaker, the time of broadcast, and the subject. The broadcast may arouse more interest if it has a provocative title.

If campaign funds are limited—and they usually are, opposition charges to the contrary—investing in five or fifteen-minute radio or TV speeches is a lot like putting all of one's eggs in one basket. Generally speaking, more is to be gained by judicious use of one-minute spots or fifteen- or thirty-second station breaks, interspersed with occasional five-minute talks. Transcriptions can also be made of all of these for use at lower rates by small town or rural stations of low wattage. The effect of repetition of these spots should be more persuasive in getting people to go to the polls and to vote for your candidates than one or two long speeches. The public is likely to dismiss the latter as just politics, whereas by dinning into their ears the date of the election and the names of your candidates, you may give them an extra impetus to stop by the polls. Once there, the tendency of many voters to vote for names with which they are familiar is well known. We will return to this later on in discussing campaign techniques.

Scatter your spots and station breaks throughout the day and the evening if you can, increasing them as election day approaches. Catch mama at the housework and papa at the evening paper.

If you are contracting for longer television periods than brief "spot" interjections during prime evening viewing time, don't—for heaven's sake don't—let the station cut in on popular situation comedies, Westerns or other expensive network type shows, which are favorites with a large part of the public. If this happens you have just lost untold potential votes. I'll never forget the howls of outrage when one of my programs preempted

"Huckleberry Hound". I hadn't realized how many friends that dog had.

As to your delivery, have a transcription made if you can afford it and ask some radio authority at your local station or a voice instructor to show you the direction in which improvements lie. Do this even though you may privately think well of your own delivery. For here is a curious thing: nearly everyone thinks that he has a good radio voice or television personality. "It ain't necessarily so."

In using a microphone in addressing a live audience, take your time in adjusting it to suit your height and speaking habits. This gradually focuses the attention of your audience, it shows them that you are in command of the situation, and it helps you to get yourself together if you happen to have a touch of mike fright. Mike fright, like stage fright, is not peculiar to you; it is best overcome (and you will overcome it as you gain experience) through familiarity with your subject. What you are after is confidence in yourself, and if you know what you are talking about and how you are going to say it, you will get along all right once well launched.

Normally you will get the best results when using a microphone by talking a few inches away from it and slightly above it. You can experiment a little in your opening remarks until you hit on the right distance. Don't clutch the mike, and don't sway back and forth around it. The audience will watch the movements of your hands and body instead of listening to your brilliant deductions.

Again, don't hesitate to stop if in doubt as to whether your voice is carrying over the hall; ask your audience if they can hear you (and if they still want to). As you warm to your subject, be careful not to shout and particularly not to shout directly into the mike. You may be disconcerted by the howling effect that sometimes results—as of a banshee wailing.

I have discovered that one's voice may be heard quite well by those in front of the mike, while those on the platform behind the speaker may be unable to hear at all although only a few feet away. This sort of dead spot is unfortunate because those on the platform with you are also the ones who, if they could only hear you, would be most likely to pay close attention. This dead spot may be due to the fact that no loudspeaker has been mounted behind those who sit behind the speaker, but whatever the cause, you can avoid the effect if you discuss the acoustics with the electrician or sound engineer before the meeting. A little attention to this detail is better than to hear later from the chairman of the meeting, "I am told that your speech was interesting, but I couldn't hear a word of it!"

As to securing publicity for political speeches, see that the local papers have advance notice of the meeting if it is felt that the occasion warrants it. If the meeting is public, a large attendance is desired. If campaign funds permit, insert advertisements several days before the meeting. Often a paid ad has the effect of stimulating the editor to do an advance news story on it and to send someone to cover the meeting. The membership of the organization sponsoring the meeting should be circularized well ahead of the meeting date.

At the meeting, if the speaker wishes to assure himself that he will be quoted accurately and wishes to select those parts of his speech that he prefers publicized, he will have available press releases not only for the local papers but for local radio and television and enough of them to go around. If it has any bearing on your political strategy whether your speech is first reported in an evening or morning newspaper, then familiarize yourself with edition deadlines; the press releases can be handed out in advance with release time noted on them if you wish.

By using a tape recorder and telephone hookups, you can sometimes work in "specials" for radio for use on news programs

107

in the form, for example, of excerpts from your speech or timed thirty-second comments. The further advantage of advance copies of news releases plus your own early arrival is that you can tape comments or answers to questions for prompt use as local news, especially if what you say is provocative or newsworthy. Being early also assures you a place in the group picture. The preferred places are on the left (your name appears first in the caption—unless the negative is reversed!) or in the center (good for people who don't like their profiles) where the rest of the group is apt to be smiling in your direction. I know a scene-stealing state senator who always thrusts his hand outward just as the picture is taken. The viewer or reader follows the hand and notices him first.

Better not plan to collect funds at a meeting where you expect to have speakers discuss issues or candidacies. Even though nothing has been said in advance about plans for fund raising, people have an instinct about those things and the size of the audience is apt to suffer noticeably. Keep the two separate; talk dollars at one meeting and sense at another.

Introducing a Speaker

The ground rules for this are not complicated. Make it snappy; all those people are out there to hear the speaker, not the man who pulls the curtain aside for the main event. So do not hog the speaker's time by chatting about yourself and your ideas on this and that or even by talking too long about the speaker. Don't try to upstage or overshadow him. You do not want to overeulogize him either to the point of embarrassment. After all, save something for his funeral oration.

Your job is to put the audience quickly into a receptive and expectant mood. Tell them a little something about the speaker, point up something warmly human about him if you can, sketch in a bit of his background, touch off a compliment or two about his attainments, and move out of the spotlight as you beckon him into it.

Notes for Chairmen and Toastmasters

If you are to preside as chairman of a meeting or toastmaster at a banquet, have the program given you before the meeting, learn something about those who will participate, and be prepared to introduce each of them with some brief, complimentary word. Throw in some jokes if you can find some that are apposite, but you will not be expected to tell a joke before each performer. Some toastmasters tend to regard the joke before each introduction as standard operating procedure, but the effect on the audience is not always felicitous.

If your meeting is built around a prominent speaker, arrange in advance to keep any other speeches short, say from five to ten minutes each. It will be easier for you to call time in these preliminary bouts if you have explained the time limits to the participants in advance.

Find an opportunity to ask your principal speaker if you can help him with any information he would like to have about the audience, the community, or any matter on which you may be able to brief him. If there are any tabooed subjects as far as that audience is concerned, he may appreciate the warning.

It is not advisable to let your meeting wear itself to a frazzle by lengthy gabbing about new business, old business, delinquent dues, and the report of the Committee on Preservation of Monuments, while the inward fires flare up in the guest of honor and slowly flicker and die. For good reason this kind of torture is classified as a slow burn. One distinguished gentleman, having long endured this inconsiderate wastage of his time, at the end of the wearying session was introduced as "the very eminent Mr. ——, who will now give you his address." The very eminent Mr. —— thereupon rose, but only to say, "My address is 1700 Elm Street, and I am going to it right away."

If your meeting is a luncheon meeting, tell the guests, about the time they are finishing their coffee, just what time you plan to bring the meeting to a close. They all think that they have business that must be attended to, and with knowledge of the closing time, they are less inclined to be restless, at least until the deadline rolls around. Furthermore, it will serve as a polite reminder to the speaker of the time limitations you trust he will observe.

There may be some in the audience or at the speaker's table whom you wish to recognize before calling on the speaker of the day. Decide in advance whether you are going to call on them for a few words or merely to take a bow; then treat all of them equally. If they are to be expected to say something, it is thoughtful to tip them off beforehand. Their impromptu remarks may be the more graceful for being a bit less impromptu.

Whenever you have entertainment scheduled as a part of your program, try to put it after the speaker. He is more apt to enjoy it then, or can leave, if he wishes. And the audience has something to stick around for. I recall a banquet of a women's club where a number of dignitaries were called on for speeches; all the vice presidents down to the sixth vice president had been heard. The audience was understandably growing restless. The toastmistress introduced the last speaker (viz., me) with these words, "Take it easy, girls, we've got just one more speaker and then you can enjoy yourselves."

You may come to share an experience common with many others who have gone before you as toastmasters; if the speaker is a success, he gets the praise; if he is a bust, you will be asked who sold you a bill of goods. And if you serve as a toastmaster many times, you may come to say with Chauncey Depew (to whom all pre-Dorothy Parker wit is customarily ascribed), "If all after dinner speakers were laid end to end—wouldn't that be nice?"

10. Political Quiz

THESE questions and answers appear here for two reasons: first, because they stand out in my mind as those which are most often posed to politicians in casual conversation, and second, because they seem to fit better in a chapter by themselves than elsewhere in this running commentary. Many other questions will doubtless occur to you, and I may discover, as I did some years ago in writing a law book, that I seem to have left out a good many more pertinent matters than I included. The penalty on that occasion was that I let myself in for quite a spate of free legal advice to other lawyers for which (instinct tells me) they were able to include something in the client's fee. What the penal obligations of the omissions here may be will doubtless develop in the near future.

I can only caution that these answers represent but my own opinion or that of those from whom I quote, with which you are free to quarrel or to differ (or to write me, suggesting some additions or corrections):

Q. What is politics?

A. Mr. Webster's dictionary defines it as "the science and art of government; the science dealing with organization, regulation, and administration of a state . . . the theory or practice of managing or directing the affairs of public policy or of political parties . . ." Walt Whitman once said of our American system, "Political democracy, as it exists and practically works in America, with all its threatening evils, supplies a training school for making first-class men. It is life's gymnasium, not of good only, but of all." Politics is the people's business, which is to say, it is your business. To say that you have no interest in politics is to say that you have no interest in government. Are you willing to let it go by default to those all too eager to take the trouble to run things for you? The end of that road turned out not to be to the liking of the people of much of Europe. It could happen anywhere. It could happen here.

Q. What is a politician?

A. Mr. Webster again: "One versed or experienced in the science of government . . ." In a republic, the powers of government are derived from the people and administered by persons holding office during the pleasure of the people who elected them, for a fixed period or during good behavior. Do you see where you come in? The extent to which your interest and experience in the science of government leads you to participate in it determine (when multiplied by others of like mind) what sort of people will be elected to office and whether they will continue to retain their power. And note that the definition for a politician applies also to a statesman. The scornful may say that "a statesman is a dead politician," but it is more truly said that a statesman lives by his principles and a politician is ruled by his interest. Much of the philosophy on which this government was founded was inspired by Jean Jacques Rousseau who observed in *The Social Contract* that "as soon as any man says of the affair of the State, 'what does it matter to me?' the State may be given up for lost." And at another place: "As soon as public service ceases to be the chief business of the citizens, and they would rather serve with their money than with their persons, the State is not far from its fall." Someone has said that America's chief weakness is that our most intelligent men are trying to operate in spite of the government instead of helping to manage it.

Q. What's wrong with politics?

A. You are. That is, if you are willing to sit in the cynic's seat and hurl the scorner's ban, if you prefer to be pharisaical about it and pass by on the other side while government is being made. That is what this book is all about, gentle reader. It is my earnest hope that I may strike a spark of interest here and there about this business of the art and science of government so that some of you, qualified by sincere purpose and a desire to lend a hand in the better operation of the political system, may be moved to do something about it. Or, at the very least, to learn enough of what goes on in politics to let your voice be heard by those who sit in the halls of government. It is said that Rome fell when, at last, "there were not Romans left to do the work of Rome."

Q. But will public officials pay any attention to me?

A. You bet they will. In the first place, they never know how many you may be multiplied by, to what extent your protest or your advice may reflect the as yet unheard voices of many others. As I have said before, you *are* public opinion. Never be hesitant about expressing your views on public matters to those who are charged with administering policy. Even if they do not appear to agree with you, they may yet be convinced by your logic or by the cumulative logic or emotion of numbers of those of you who feel the same way. There are not many lost causes. Most of them have been mislaid and lie neglected, through apathy or discouragement. Not all causes deserve to succeed, it is true. But truth has a better chance when its advocates are courageous—and persistent.

Q. Why should I bother to vote?

A. Why should you bother to shave? Is it not as important to keep your government clean as it is your face? I have a friend who says, as he drops his ballot into the box, "Now I have earned my right to criticize my government." Your vote is important not alone because you are sharing in turning the wheels of government, but your failure to vote, when cumulated

113

by others similarly lackadaisical, leaves the operation of public business by default to those who may, for selfish purposes, operate that government greatly to your detriment and to the disadvantage of the whole people. And you can never be sure how important your single vote may prove to be. We have all read of elections that were won or lost by a half-dozen votes—or by one. It may have been yours. There have been many instances of elections where less than one vote per precinct represented the narrow margin of victory.* I recall a recent election that was undoubtedly won in the last half hour the polls were open as a result of the efforts of volunteer workers who brought out an average of ten additional voters per precinct by phone calls and personal visits. Analysis revealed that most of them had been sitting at home reading the paper or playing with the children, with never a thought of the election or of the issues at stake. On not voting, let me borrow from Joseph Fouché, who said in another connection, "It is more than a crime; it is a political fault."

Q. Why should I bother to vote at the primary election?

A. Don't you want something better than the lesser of two evils? That is the kind of selection you may find yourself making at the general election, when no interest has been shown at the primaries in the selection of party candidates. For it is in the primary elections that the poltical parties choose up sides, except in those states where party candidacies are determined in state conventions, in which latter case your influence should be exerted in the selection of delegates to these conventions. It is too late to complain at the general elections about your choice between Tweedledum and Tweedledee. Tweedledum got one nomination because his supporters were on the job and they figured you wouldn't be. And, by a strange coincidence, that

---

* Hindsight is said to be 20/20 but this line was first written in 1946. I later won an election by less than that margin!—Author.

s how Tweedledee got the other. It is a common mistake to underestimate the importance of primary elections, to regard them as preliminary skirmishes, a warmup for the main bout in the fall. More often the primary is the real thing because the caliber of the respective candidates put forward as intended party designees may depend upon the degree of public participation to be expected at the primary. Of course, it is also the only opportunity offered to dissident citizens to displace an incompetent favorite by entering an opponent for whom superior qualifications can be claimed. To vote in the general election and ignore the primary makes as much sense as to eat the shell and throw the nut away.

Q. Do I have to belong to a party? What difference does it make?

A. No. No one can require you to belong to a political party. The decision is entirely up to you. You will be asked, upon registration as a voter, whether you wish to designate yourself as a member of a political party or as a nonpartisan. Some citizens prefer to keep their voting preferences secret for personal or business reasons. Others call themselves nonpartisan because of a desire to maintain their independent status or because, at least for the time being, they are just shopping around and have not settled on a political preference. As to what difference it makes whether one belongs to a party or not, there is some disqualification in being registered "nonpartisan" or "no party" in most jurisdictions; such a registrant is barred from participating in primary elections. In the great American game of choosing up rival teams, the aloof nonpartisan is relegated to a bystander's role. To my mind such a disqualification is a serious one; the primary election decision is precisely the one wherein the plain citizen can least afford to toss away his opportunity to influence the choice of candidates. The average American's predilection for being on, or rooting for, the team of his choice is evidenced by the fact that the number of voters registered as without party affiliation is a very small percentage of the whole.

Q. To register as a voter, what do I do?

A. If you wish to register for any reason (for example, you have just come of age, returned from military service, changed your name by marriage or changed your residence), you can find out how and where to register by inquiry of the division committeeman of either party or at the county courthouse or city hall. The registration books are open at certain hours and on certain days and are kept by officials variously known as registration commissioners, county commissioners, assessors, or election board members. Registration, depending on state laws, may be permanent, *i.e.,* good until lost by change of address, lapse of time, failure to exercise, or other limiting factors; or you may be required to register every year or every two or four years. State, not federal, law will govern this. The same sources can also inform you whether your state has any special registration requirements, and whether and under what circumstances one may vote by absentee ballot. In some jurisdictions registrars will visit your home to record you as a registered elector, in others provision is made for traveling registrars to sit in various localities on specified days, or you may be permitted to register up to a specified day or a specified deadline before election dates at the registration offices designated by law. In any event, it will be advisable for you to inform yourself what you must do in order to assure your right to vote at forthcoming elections.

Q. Can I vote for one party if I am registered as a member of another party?

A. Yes, in the general election. Once in the voting booth you are alone with your conscience. The two of you can vote any way you wish.

In primary elections, some states permit voters to "cross over" without restriction to the candidates of one's own party. Most states do not.

Q. Can I vote for some candidates in one party and some in the other?

A. Yes, except where ruled out in certain primaries. You may split your ticket, voting for candidates without regard to their or your party designation, so long as you do not vote for more candidates than are to be elected to designated offices. That will invalidate your ballot; if you are using a voting machine, most of them are so constructed as not to permit you to vote for more candidates than is legally permissible. It is a matter of general knowledge among politicians that many voters in a general election, where a straight party preference is offered, will not as a rule split their tickets. They may vote a straight party ticket, either through preference for that procedure or because (and this is especially true where voting machines are used) he or she becomes confused by the multiple marking or lever pulling involved in split voting, and the dilemma is resolved by making the party crosses or pulling the party lever. Wherever a marked amount of split voting occurs, it is usually safe to conclude that some issue or candidacy has aroused the electorate to an unusual degree. Latterly, independent voting is on the increase. In my state, in some elections, more than one third of those voting have split their tickets. If a candidate shows exceptional strength by drawing a number of individual votes from the other party via the split-ticket route, he has established in the political mind one of two conclusions: either he is a remarkable vote getter (and not to be lost sight of when votes are needed on some future occasion) or some of the political workers have arranged some ticket cutting in his favor. In some states, voters may be challenged at primary elections by watchers or election officials if it is believed that they have (at a previous election) voted for a majority (or in some states for any) of the candidates of the party other than that in which the voter is registered. The voter may then be required to take an affidavit to the contrary to qualify himself for voting in the primary election where so challenged. Challenges are used rather sparingly, save where the contest is unusually heated, because of the danger of alienating the voter.

Q. How does the candidate get his name on the ballot?

A. In the primary election (as distinguished from states where candidates are selected in conventions) this is usually accomplished by filing a petition for the office, signed by the number of qualified electors required by law, signed or verified (or both) by the candidate, and filed in the office designated for the receipt of nominating petitions, accompanied by the filing fee where one is required.

Nominating petitions are required to be filed a stated number of days before the primary election. Ordinarily they bear substantially more than the minimum number of names required, since the petitioning voters are subject to challenge as nonresidents, not registered in the same party as the candidate or for other reasons stated in the election laws. These laws also fix the deadline within which a candidate may withdraw his petition for nomination since candidates are often withdrawn when some other candidate has received assurances of party support, or for other reasons.

At the general election the names on the ballot are those of the candidates nominated by the respective parties in the primary election or placed on the ballot by party committees or conventions where permitted by state laws.

In some states, candidates defeated in primary elections may file on independent or preempted tickets, in others they may not. Likewise, in New York and Vermont candidates may file and be nominated on more than one party ticket while in other states cross-filing is prohibited or permitted only in the case of candidates for judicial office.

In some jurisdictions, candidates are required by party regulation or state law to take an oath in advance of the primary to abide by the result of the primary election. Again, in some states, candidates are permitted to insert a symbol, slogan, or short statement of principles accompanying their names on the ballot or they may state whether they are the present incumbents of the office seeking reelection. In other states only the names of the candidates appear in the columns bearing the party designation.

Q. How can I get information about the candidates and for what they stand?

A. In the time of the Roman Republic the seekers after office appeared in the Forum and market place dressed in white to signify their purity of purpose. The Latin word for one so attired was *candidatus*, hence candidate. Judging from the frequency with which this question is asked, the matter of judging the relative purity of candidates is, to many voters, a baffling one. The gap between the pledge and the performance has so often seemed such a veritable chasm as to generate skepticism when faced by these bright new promises. Yet there are numerous ways by which you may assay these political ores for gold or dross.

You may discuss the candidates with your local committeemen, in which case you will doubtless make due allowance for possible bias; nevertheless you may find out a good deal of that which you want to know. Political leaders or politically conscious citizens whose judgment you respect will be glad to give advice and are complimented because you have consulted them.

There are in many communities nonpartisan citizens and voters' groups that collect and compile information about candidates and concerning issues to be voted on. Some of

119

their information may have been derived from replies to questionnaires submitted by the candidates. A word of warning here: The more truly nonpartisan the group the more reliable the information furnished would seem to be. But a number of pressure groups with special interests to serve also use questionnaires, and their questions are sometimes loaded to reflect a particular ideology and to favor their preselected candidates who can more readily answer the carefully chosen questions. Thus they gain the recommendation of the pressure group, which has been promised sometimes in advance of the questionnaire mailing. Other candidates may ignore these questionnaires and their failure to answer may not in itself be an argument against such a candidate. Remember, the candidate may receive scores of questionnaires; he must decide which ones deserve a reply.

There are other ways for the inquisitive voter to glean information: attendance at political meetings to size up the seekers after public favor face to face, listening to radio-TV talks, reading the papers, the editorials as well as the news items (again allowing for the possible bias of the newswriter or of the newspaper); but it seems to me that the best way to get information about a candidate is to ask the candidate himself. Chances are he will be in public sight a good deal during the campaign. He is asking you to hire him for the job. Ask him why he thinks he can do the work. It is not as difficult to question candidates as you may think. Most office seekers are easily approachable. If he is not, that is a point against him.

In making up your mind, what do you want to know about the candidate before you come to cast your vote? Well, who are his associates? What is their background? What is his past record? Is he known as one who keeps his promises? Has he been active in civic, charitable, or neighborhood affairs? What is his business, labor or professional reputation? What did he do during wartime? If he has held office before, how did he conduct himself? What are his personal habits? Is he forthright or secretive? Is he levelheaded? What views has he expressed on public questions? Public office is a public trust, said Grover Cleveland; is the candidate the kind of person who would feel that way about it?*

One manufacturer sells salt with the slogan: "When it rains, it pours." When a candidate's promises rain down too literally for your digestion, pour a little salt on each. Lastly, use at least as much care in judging public servants as you would in appraising a race horse. Consider his antecedents. Is he by Greed out of Corruption or by Honesty out of High Purpose? You have more to lose at the polls than at the races.

Q. Who counts the votes?

A. I have heard it said that the winners do. It sometimes happens that way where corrupt county and city machine organizations are still dominant; I believe that most political observers will agree with me that dishonest vote counting is steadily decreasing in this country. Increasing intelligence of the electorate and the advent of voting machines (which, however, are not infallible), together with rising public interest in the prosecution of vote frauds, have tended to reduce that form of crookedness to the status of a sore thumb exception. State laws differ considerably as to how ballots shall be counted; they should be consulted for detailed information.

Generally speaking, the ballots are first counted, after the polls are closed, in the polling place by the election officers serving in the precinct. Their tallies are usually checked by the election judges, election officers, or watchers present and delivered to the county or city election office, where an official

---

* Ironically, President Cleveland admitted having fathered an illegitimate child. "Ma, ma, ma, where's my pa?" cried the Republicans. "Gone to the White House, ha, ha, ha!" answered the Democrats.

public count is conducted at a later date. In some states, *e.g.*, Kentucky, ballots are not counted first at the polls, but the count comes a short time later at the central election offices. State laws also provide methods for challenging votes at the polls, in court on election day, and at the official vote count, as well as for a recount if decreed by proper authority on proof properly presented.

Q. Do public officials pay any attention to public-opinion polls?

A. If he is an elected public official, interested in what people are thinking or in retaining his office, or both, he is quite likely to follow public opinion polls with lively interest, especially since the better known public opinion services have improved their techniques and have established reputations for moderately accurate results, *as of the time the poll is taken.* One respected and successful pollster relies on about 400 carefully selected interviews in depth for a statewide poll, even in a large state. The 1948 results, regarded as evidence of the inaccuracy of the polls, brought to light faulty techniques including failure to evaluate the "undecided" vote, the turnout at the polls of various voting groups, laxness in checking on voters right up to election day. Polls may be a guide to the outcome, but they are far from infallible. There is sometimes an interaction here; the public opinion polls may lead public officials who are policy makers to adopt certain decisions that, in turn, may cause public opinion to veer in a direction somewhat different from that represented at the time of the last poll sampling. Sometime ago Dr. Gallup spoke to an evening gathering of some sixty members of Congress, each of whom was permitted to ask him one question at the end of his talk. After explaining the precautions taken to secure an accurate sampling of economic, political, racial, religious, and other groupings, using generally from 3,000 to 30,000 poll takers on questions of national interest, the question period—the opportunity to poll Dr. Gallup —began. And here is the answer to your question: Every one of the sixty Congressmen had a question for the doctor! They ranged from unqualified approval to open skepticism by one or two present, but the lively interest in opinion polls was undeniable on the part of men who must be good judges of public opinion in their own right if they are to retain public confidence. Incidentally, every public official on each trip home fancies himself as a walking Gallup Poll. In point of fact, candidates and incumbents often order their own polls and surveys from professional opinion research groups.

These polls are less expensive when only a typical town, county or precinct is polled in a test-tube survey. Of course, a poll of your whole constituency may be more revealing.

Polls are useful indicators not only of what voters are likely to do *as of the time the poll is taken* but may reveal what issues or actions are of major concern. Prevailing appraisals of the candidates, their assets and liabilities, can also be brought to light. However, polls do not always reveal the *intensity* of voter approval or disapproval.

More and more, polls are taken immediately after a news break affecting the campaign or after a public debate between candidates to gauge public reaction.

An argument can be made that polls do (if properly taken) reflect sentiment as of the time of the interviews, but it must be borne in mind that not all of the public will enter the voting booths (percentages of voter interest vary with poltical, economic and social groups) and the pollster can never be sure how the undecided or (heretofore) apathetic group will break. An in-depth survey is an important way to find out what is "bugging" voters, so that you can wage your campaign on issues that appeal.

Q. Does it do any good to write to my congressman? (or senator? or county supervisor? or councilman?)

A. It does. In the first place, you will feel better after you get it off your chest. The real implication of the question, however, may be restated thus: Does correspondence between public officials and their constituents play any part in advancing the public welfare? When you write to your legislator or local official you are helping his public opinion poll. You are contributing your sample. Letters from constituents ordinarily receive careful attention. They are frequently mulled over and compared with other correspondence on the same subject or with letters received by colleagues from their constituents. If you leaf through the appendix of the Congressional Record, nearly every day you will find included letters to members from their voters at home. Most of them are not from rich or powerful personages in the usual usage of the term but from plain citizens, rich in common sense and powerful because the legislators know that for one who writes in a certain vein there may be hundreds or thousands who harbor similar opinions.

In writing, it is your own thoughts and your own way of reasoning out a viewpoint that count. Such a letter will receive far more consideration than hundreds of form letters or canned telegrams. Most of these latter move from letter opener to wastebasket, barely touching the desk top in their unconsidered passage. And the average public official can spot a form letter every time.

Your letter will gain effectiveness if it adopts a reasonable, fair-minded approach; vituperation and violent language set up resentment and butter no parsnips. If you must be critical, if you must call your official to account, do so, assigning your reasons, but give him credit for acting from proper motives (unless you can prove the fact to be otherwise, without much room for doubt) as you will wish to be given credit for the same propriety of motive in advancing your own contention. If you must be critical as to a given matter, try to find room to praise your recipient for some other action of his if you can. Most public officials learn, in time, to discount bald flattery for what it is, but so little considered praise comes their way that it may well come as a surprise. While his guard comes down, your arguments may find their mark. It is also thoughtful to indicate whether an answer is desired, as such a notation is a timesaver to a busy individual.

Type your letter if you can. Handwritten letters, especially long illegible ones, go to the bottom of the pile or to someone in the office to translate. Also, write to the office of a public official, not to his home. His office at the state or national capital may be distant from his home and you simply delay an answer. Even if home and office are in the same city, you do not get the special attention you're fishing for, since the official will nearly always take a batch of such letters to the office to be opened. This generally puts this type of mail at the bottom of the pile of those already prepared for the official's attention.

For maximum effectiveness, write only when you have something constructive to say. Do not pelt or pester public officials with a series of utter trivialities, popping off like a string of Chinese firecrackers. At a recent school of political techniques, a radical woman speaker, presenting herself as an expert on the subject of influencing legislation, proposed that legislators be buried under hundreds of letters and telegrams all advocating the same proposal. They should also receive, she burbled on, frequent telephone calls, preferably at dinnertime, demanding the desired action. If the lady drew any pay for that advice, she ought to be prosecuted for obtaining money under false pretenses. I cannot imagine any procedure more ill advised or more likely to drain off any residue of good will that may have existed prior to this frenetic onslaught.

What was said about getting to know candidates for public office likewise has application here. As your legislator may be functioning at some distance from you, much of the time you can only communicate your ideas to him by correspondence. But when circumstances permit, there is no substitute for direct man-to-man exchange of views. There will be many calls upon his time, and it would be unreasonable to demand more than a fair amount of it. The average person in public life will be glad to have a chance to talk to you—the first time. After that, it will depend a good bit on you and on the impression you have made. For better or worse, every public official must decide how much time he may allot to each of the demands upon him. Yet, the ablest public men I know seem, somehow, to be able to find time to listen to any person who really has something worth saying.

Q. How do I get a copy of a legislative bill?

A. There are state and federal officials who will furnish you with legislative bills, usually the clerk of the legislative body in which it was introduced, or where it is pending if it has not been enacted into law. By long-standing custom, bills are generally obtained by state and federal legislators upon request of constituents. This is one of the many assignments for which legislators expect to be called upon during their attendance at the sessions at the state capitol or in Washington. Technically, a bill becomes an act when it has been adopted by the house so referring to it, but in common understanding an act is a bill that has passed through all the legislative and executive processes that may be required for its final enactment, at which point it becomes a public law. Only a small percentage of bills introduced ever become law, for which Allah be praised.

Q. May I attend hearings of legislative committees?

A. Yes, where the hearings are public as distinguished from closed sessions, sometimes called executive sessions. If it is not customary for notice of public hearings to be carried in local newspapers (a morning paper lists them in Washington), you may get this information from the clerk of the legislative committee or from your legislator, either of whom can also tell you the location of the hearing room. If you wish to testify before a legislative committee, you may put your request directly to the chairman or the ranking minority member of the committee, to any member of the committee, to the committee clerk, or to your representative in that legislative body. Whether you will then be invited to testify may depend on whether the committee or its chairman decides that what you have to offer is pertinent to the proceedings. A reading of some committee hearings leads one to wonder whether considerable latitude has not been permitted in determining who shall be heard. But in the interest of democratic procedure it is probably far better to err in this direction than in the other.

Q. What is lobbying?

A. The activity of one or more persons in attempting to influence the course of legislation. The Federal Regulation of Lobbying Act of 1946, in defining who shall register as lobbyists, describes the persons to whom applicable as follows:

. . . any person except a political committee as defined in the Federal Corrupt Practices Act, and duly organized State or local committees of a political party), who by himself, or through any agent or employee or other persons in any manner whatsoever, directly or indirectly, solicits, collects, or receives money or any other thing of value to be used principally to aid, or the principal purpose of which person is to aid, in the accomplishment of any of the following purposes:
  (a) The passage or defeat of any legislation by the Congress of the United States.
  (b) To influence, directly or indirectly, the passage or defeat of any legislation by the Congress of the United States.

127

The federal law is thus aimed at the registration of lobbyists who are paid for that purpose or who solicit or use money in lobbying activities.

The word lobbyist has been used so often in a derogatory sense that it has acquired an unpleasant connotation, but in practice everyone who takes a proper interest as a citizen in urging upon legislators the passage or defeat of any proposal is engaged in a form of lobbying. Lobbying may be useful in improving, promoting, delaying, or defeating legislation. Lobbyists may supply legislators with information or research that is highly beneficial. The Constitution of the United States wisely provides that "Congress shall make no law respecting . . . the right of the people peaceably to assemble and to petition the Government for a redress of grievances." So one may lobby, but if one is paid for it, one must register before engaging in federal lobbying. Some states have laws concerning registration of lobbyists. Of course, the term itself comes from the lobbies or passages in the neighborhood of legislative halls, often the strategic location for buttonholing a legislator.

Q. What is logrolling?

A. Perhaps best described as "you vote for my bill and I'll vote for yours": the process by which legislative support is secured for a bill by offering, in return, to assist in the passage of legislation desired by other legislators. It is not the highest type of statesmanship, perhaps, but as almost all legislation is enacted by a process of compromise to meet varying objections interposed, it is not surprising that efforts are made to eliminate the obstacles as they arise. Quids are expected for quos. This form of legislative back-scratching reminds one of the Chinese proverb, "don't shout unless you are sure of an echo."

Q. What is a liberal? A conservative?

A. Dictionary definitions are not much help here. Webster says a liberal is "an opponent of conservatism," also, "one who advocates extension of freedom in political institutions." Mr. Webster is no more help when he wrestles with a conservative: "one opposed to hasty changes in the political, religious, or civil institutions of the country." Alas for Mr. Webster, these labels have come to mean whatever we or our opponents want them to mean at any given time. Those who are opposed to hasty changes believe that theirs is the true liberalism since it demands that we hold fast to the freedoms guaranteed by the Founding Fathers. Those who oppose conservatism often advocate continued extension of governmental controls, which seem to limit rather than to extend freedom in political institutions. And if a conservative is one "opposed to hasty changes in political . . . institutions", is a liberal one in favor of hasty changes?

It depends so much on who uses the term and its inward meaning to the user. To himself, a liberal is the champion of the dignity of man; to his adversary, he is a radical. To himself, the conservative is the protector of the guaranteed rights of the individual; to his critic, he is a reactionary. And the same thing happens when you try to get away from it all by using somewhat different terms, such as progressive, middle-of-the-road, moderate or centrist.*

In speaking to students of political science as a guest lecturer, I have been asked, "Is it better to be a liberal or a conservative in politics?" It has been easy for me to vault between the horns of that dilemma because I believe that one should avoid hanging an ideological label on oneself. My advice is to avoid labels. Be a reasoning, thinking human being even though it may lead you to adopt what is regarded as a liberal attitude on one question, while your views on another may appear to be of a conservative cast. The apparent inconsistency here is not real if you have

---

* Former President Eisenhower has described himself, in a letter to me, as a "constructive centrist."

arrived at each conclusion by a balanced heart-and-head approach.

One who declares himself before the world as a conservative or as a liberal is cutting ruts in his brain. He is preparing the way to condition himself to believe in certain things because they have been classified as conservative or liberal approaches. Hang an ideological label on yourself, bind yourself in advance to swallow its nostrums, and you will be led around by the nose by the high priests of political liberalism or conservatism. The ruts are at the *side* of the road. There is a more level patch in the center! Think for yourself; do the leading instead of the following.

There are plenty of seats up front!

11. The Care and Feeding of Legislation

How do the members of a legislative body know what legislation is needed by state or nation? How does one bring ideas about legislation to the attention of legislators? How does a bill get to be a law? All of these questions and many more confront those charged by their election to legislative office with the care and feeding of legislative brain children.

Upon the convening of a legislative session, the possibility of a dearth of suggested legislation is the least of a legislator's worries. For every proposal that has the slightest chance of being enacted into law there are ten or a dozen or a hundred that may never get into bill form, or if they do, are destined to languish forever in the dark recesses of the committee to which they have been consigned. Suggestions beginning "there ought to be a law . . ." pour in from labor and business, from veterans, farmers, women's clubs, doctors, lawyers, and Indian chiefs. More laws are suggested by newspapers, television and radio commentators—those medicine men of the air waves— and advertisers; resolutions come in from conventions, rallies, and clambakes; petitions roll in, some from individuals and some bearing signatures a mile long. And practically no one ever organizes a movement to repeal the thousands of unnecessary laws we have on the books.

Then there is the legislative program of the administration in power, whose measures are introduced by its recognized spokesmen. These bills, generally speaking, have the best chance of passage through both houses of the legislature. (Only Nebraska has a unicameral, or single-house, legislative body.) Many bills may also be introduced at the request of local political leaders or on the initiative of individual members in pursuit of some program in which they are interested.

Still other bills are introduced by the minority leadership in furtherance of their political and legislative plans. These necessarily have less chance of success than majority-sponsored legislation, but enough votes may be picked up from the majority side or by the alignment of blocs sharing a common interest in a specific proposal, or the measure may succeed because of a flare-up of public opinion in its favor. Where it appears that a minority-sponsored proposal is likely to pass, it is not unusual for the majority to attempt to seize credit by introducing an identical or closely similar bill, under the name of a majority member, the substitute bill then being given the green light for passage.

Senior legislators of the same party are not always above using a like device when a junior member is discovered in possession of some popular vote-nourishing tidbit; the law of the legislative jungle is ofttime harsh. On one occasion, the State Bar Association Criminal Law Committee, of which I was then Chairman, prepared a much-needed bill providing for voluntary waiver of jury trials in criminal cases in order to expedite the work of the criminal courts. After the draft had been placed in the hands of an able lawmaker of the majority party and the bill introduced by him, considerable public support developed as it became evident that fewer jurors would have to be summoned and paid for by the counties. The bill, introduced by an older member, was soon displaced on the legislative calendar by another, identical except for one weakening and limiting clause apparently inserted without much thought. The bill passed in that form over the objection of the Bar Association Committee; it took nearly ten years to get an amendment passed to eliminate the one objectionable and unnecessary line.

Most bills are introduced by individual legislators for purposes which may be quite broad or which may be limited to a narrow special purpose of relief or correction. In the U.S. Senate, bills offered by a Senator may be cosponsored, with his permission, by any number of Senators who thus indicate their interest and support. In the U.S. House of Representatives cosponsorship is not permitted, so members get around that block quite readily by introducing identical bills.

Suppose you have some ideas about legislation, whether pending or not yet introduced, how do you bring your views to the attention of legislators? The great British statesman, Edmund Burke, in his Speech to the Electors of Bristol on November 3rd, 1774, recited what may be taken to be the ideal qualification of a receptive legislator. If all were to fit the mold, happy indeed would be the lot of their constituents. As one reads Burke's words, it is easy to comprehend the hold he had on his own constituency and the respect with which his speeches were listened to in his own country and here across the waters:

> It ought to be the happiness and glory of a representative to live in the strictest union, the closest correspondence, and the most unreserved communication with his constituents. Their wishes ought to have great weight with him; their opinion high respect; their business unremitted attention. It is his duty to sacrifice his repose, his pleasures, his satisfaction, to theirs; and above all, ever, and in all cases, to prefer their interests to his own.

Notice that Edmund Burke spoke of preferring the interests of his constituents to his own; he did not mean their views necessarily nor their opinions merely. Hear him on that:

> . . . Your representative owes you, not his industry only, but his judgment; and he betrays instead of serving you if he sacrifices it to your opinion.

If you have something on your mind about legislation that you believe deserving of consideration, there is no reason why you should not write or talk to your representative in the state or federal legislature about it. You may be sure that others have been discussing with him throughout the session their opinions on proposed or pending bills. The chances are that you will find your representative approachable and interested. You are likely to find him as easy to talk to as the corner druggist or your local newspaper editor. In fact, they may be one and the same person. For the state and federal legislatures are made up for the most part of average citizens, of whom some may exceed the rest in statesmanly stature and some may drag along in the ruck. Generally, their reactions and their judgments are in no way extraordinary or Olympian. In a republic, they are chosen by the people from among their own number to devise the rules under which free men may conduct their affairs in security and with respect for the rights of others.

To one who had written to a national magazine expressing the hope that some day "our Congress may be composed of men of brilliance; there is a woeful lack of genius among its membership," a young lady composed this riposte: "We should be glad that our Representatives are a cross section of the population; if they were all geniuses, my Congressman wouldn't represent *me*!" The lady has a point.

The United States Constitution guarantees the right of petition for redress of grievances. Any person or group of people may address a petition to the Congress, which any member is privileged to introduce for them. Such petitions appear in the Congressional Record, together with a brief summary of their content. Most states have similar provisions for petitions to state legislatures. And often suggestions made to state legislators result in the legislature of a state memorializing the federal Congress, soliciting attention to a specified measure or project.

It is true that the interest of a single individual is rarely sufficient to bring about action on legislation (although there have been successful one-man or one-women lobbies at times). An effort to secure the enactment of legislation has a better chance of success when pressed by a number of people working toward the same goal, whether through an organization formed for that specific purpose or through a trade association, labor union legislative committee, farm, veteran, church or other groups of citizens having a mutual interest in the passage or defeat of legislation affecting their welfare. It is common practice for such groups to write or to interview their representatives either as members of the organization or acting through agents designated by them for the purpose. There are, of course, many powerful and energetic lobbies that are sleeplessly operating to influence the passage or defeat of legislation. Some of these maintain full-time paid staffs in Washington and in the state capitals. Some keep their offices in their hats.

Often both individuals and pressure groups interest themselves in attempting to create a favorable or unfavorable climate as the case may be, toward pending or rumored legislative action. Aside from interviews and correspondence, this may also take the form of inducing editorial comment, letters to the editors of newspapers, securing the expression of opinion by radio, television, and news commentators (do not think it isn't done!), procuring the passage of resolutions by various organizations, billboard advertising, car cards, speeches, circulars, charts, pickets, and even sandwich men. Nor is pressure upon political associates or personal friends neglected.

Action to influence legislation is not confined to persuasion directed to the individual legislator but extends to hearings in legislative committees through testimony or the furnishing of briefs, research information, editorials, letters, petitions, and memorials. If the measure is finally enacted, pressure for its approval or disapproval shifts to the governor or the president. If the measure is vetoed, pressure for sustaining or overriding the veto shifts back to the legislature.

It should not be inferred that action to influence legislation is per se reprehensible. Far from being an unworthy activity, the presentation of arguments pro and con, if conducted in open and aboveboard fashion, is a desirable extension of the democratic process. By subjecting proposals to the closest scrutiny, error may be discovered, fallacies may be run to earth, and the public welfare better served. Structural defects had better be discovered before the projected addition is built onto the house of government.

In the federal Congress a distinction exists between public bills and private bills.

Public bills concern the general public interest and, if enacted, are codified into the Public Laws of the United States where they may be found in the United States Code. They become, unless repealed, modified by later statutes or declared unconstitutional by the Supreme Court, a continuing part of the general law of the land.

The governor of every state, except North Carolina, may veto legislation. Forty-two states permit a partial or "item" veto.

Private bills may be defined as bills for the relief or special benefit of an individual or a local governmental unit. Those presented in Congress mainly concern claims against the Government or confer the right to bring a court action. Since the passage of the Federal Tort Claims Act in 1946, jurisdiction of most private tort (i.e., damage) claims against the government is transferred from the Congress to the executive agency concerned and the federal courts. A number of other private claims are also removed from Congressional consideration, which should relieve the federal legislature of a considerable burden.

Also removed from the private domain of Congress are bills for construction of a bridge across a navigable stream and bills to correct a military, naval or air force record. The main type of private bills presently concerning a legislator are special immigration bills to permit entry of individuals, to confer lawful resident status on persons otherwise subject to deportation or to confer jurisdiction upon federal courts to hear claims against the U.S., or controversies involving U.S. officials or agencies otherwise barred by lapse of time or because of statutory inhibitions.

The legislatures of a number of states are forbidden by constitutional provisions to enact local or special legislation. In those where there is no such prohibition, it is a safe bet that many members of their legislative bodies would welcome such a constitutional bar.

The pressure for enactment of public bills comes from citizens generally, organizations and communities affected, trade and labor groups, farm and veterans representatives, from all and sundry who sense weal or woe to their specialized interests. In the case of private bills, the chief interest in their passage is generated by the individual, group, or locality affected, which means much less pressure on the lawmakers for such measures considered singly; yet the total steam behind a multitude of private bills may exceed the activity centered on public legislation. As the amount at stake or result desired in a private bill is comparatively minor (except in bills conferring jurisdiction on courts to hear claims), as compared with the impact of general legislation, the opposition arising may be proportionately less.

Ironically, the political rewards of passage of private immigration bills may be appreciably greater than many public bills involving more legislative application because of the gratitude of reunited families (or ethnic clans). Legislators do not shun favorable publicity and enhanced reputation for caring about the troublous affairs of distressed people. Few human interest stories tug at the heart more than that of an aged mother reunited with her children after decades of separation.

The procedure involved in the passage of a bill through the legislature is much the same in the state and federal governments, and therefore a general picture of the journey of a measure from idea to law can be gained from an examination of the progress of a typical bill originating in the U.S. House of Representatives.

The suggestion for the introduction of the bill is made to a member by the administration or one of its agencies, by party leaders, the ranking member on his committee, or by interested citizens, or the member conceives of the need for legislation on a given subject.

The bill is then drafted by the legislator, who may enlist for this purpose the services of executive agencies or of the Office of the Legislative Council, whose facilities and staff have been increased by the Legislative Reorganization Act of 1946.

A House bill then goes through the following stages: *

a) Introduction by a member, by placing the measure in the hopper, a box on the clerk's desk; it is numbered and sent to the Government Printing Office and made available next morning at the document room.

b) Reference to the proper standing or select committee— public bills and bills coming from the Senate by the parliamentarian under direction of the speaker; private bills on recommendation of the member.

c) Report from committee—usually after hearing, either before the full committee or before a subcommittee.

d) Placing on the calendar—according to its classification as a revenue bill, private bill, etc. Occasionally a privileged bill is considered as soon as reported.

e) Consideration in Committee of the Whole, if on the Union Calendar—including general debate and reading for amendment, with speeches limited to five minutes.

---

* *Our American Government* (1963 Edition). U.S. Government Printing Office (Senate Document No. 10).

f) Second reading and consideration in the House—in the case of bills considered in Committee of the Whole, the second reading is had in committee. In either case, the bill is open to amendment after the second reading.

g) Engrossment and third reading by title only—the question is put by the speaker as being then in order and decided at one vote. A negative vote at this stage defeats the bill as completely as a [negative] vote on passage.

h) Passage—the question of the passage being put by the Speaker automatically without motion from the floor.

i) Transmission to the Senate, by message.

j) Consideration by the Senate—usually after reference to and report from committee, reading, debate, and opportunity for amendment.

k) Return from Senate with or without amendment—if the Senate rejects the bill, it so notifies the House.

l) Consideration of Senate amendments by the House—either agreeing, agreeing with amendment or disagreeing with each amendment separately.

m) Settlement of differences by a joint conference, which usually consists of the senior members of both parties on the committees or subcommittees in each chamber who have jurisdiction over a given bill. The conference report must be approved by both houses of Congress. If rejected by either house, it cannot be amended. Where a conference report has been so rejected, each body must determine whether it will again go into conference with the other. Either or both houses may instruct their conferees to insist upon their version of the bill or upon specific amendments. This process continues until conferees of both houses have agreed and both houses have accepted finally the conference report.

n) Enrollment on parchment paper.

o) Examination by the appropriate authority in each House responsible for seeing that the bills are properly enrolled (the Committee on House Administration in the House and the Secretary of the Senate in the Senate), the Chairman of the House Committee and the Secretary of the Senate certifying as to each House or Senate bill examined respectively that it has been found truly enrolled and the certifying as to origin by the Clerk of the House as to House bills and the Secretary of the Senate as to Senate bills.

p) Signing—by the Speaker first in all cases, then by the president of the Senate.

q) Transmittal to the President of the United States.

r) Approval or disapproval by the President—usually after referring it to the department affected for recommendation. Where the President disapproves, he may exercise his veto power. For a number of years it has been generally accepted that the President's time period of ten days (Sundays excepted) in which to exercise his veto power does not run until the measure has actually been received at the White House. Thus a friendly majority party could delay on Capitol Hill formal and final engrossment of a bill to give the President more time.

In many cases where bills have been sent to the President toward the close of a session, he has taken advantage of the Constitutional provision stating that if, within these ten days, Congress adjourns and so prevents the return of a bill to which the President objects, that bill does not become law. Thus, he has held until after adjournment measures of which he disapproved but which for some reason he did not wish to return with his objections to Congress for further action. This is the so-called pocket veto.

s) Action on a bill vetoed—the House or Senate may consider the veto message at once, postpone consideration of the message to a certain day, or refer the same to a committee. If it fails to pass the House to which returned, by a two-thirds vote, no further action is taken. The President returns the vetoed bill to the House in which it originated which then has the first crack at it. To become law after veto, it must pass both houses by a two-thirds vote.

t) Filing with the Administrator of the General Services Administration for deposit in the Archives.

In the Senate, under recent practices, nearly all bills are introduced by dropping them into a hopper at the presiding officer's desk. A few of them are still introduced from the floor by the senator's rising in his place, saying, "Mr. President", and waiting for the presiding officer to recognize him. The latter does so by saying, "The Senator from ——", naming the state from which the senator hails. Then the senator states that he desires to introduce a bill or sundry bills and usually discusses his proposals. A senator may introduce a bill from the floor at any time except during a quorum call or roll call by obtaining unanimous consent for that purpose.

Bills do not ordinarily pass by strict party vote as some may think. Once the legislative body has organized itself for business by selection of a Speaker (from the majority party) and of the majority and minority leaders, a procedure which is always by strict party vote, the members rarely thereafter stay within rigid party lines when voting.

True, general party lines are often ascertainable on roll calls (perhaps more regularly in state legislatures than in the Congress), but the divergent interests of industrial, urban, suburban and rural areas or other cleavages (generally economic) lead to the formation of blocs. A bloc is an aggregation of legislators who may act together for a common purpose, transcending, to that extent, party allegiance.

Strict party votes occur at times when the parties have bound themselves to abide by the results of their separate party caucuses or conferences.

The efforts of a political party to carry out its program are discernible as one studies the sum total of legislative roll calls, from which the adherence of the greater number of members of the party on a given issue or line of policy may be noted. But on most roll calls, there is some straying from the party fold on both sides of the aisle.

There is far less party discipline, other than the discipline of conscience or public opinion, in the U.S. Congress than in the British Parliament where a "three line whip" notice (i.e., underlined three times in the notice to all members) is disregarded at the member's peril. When a vote of confidence follows a "three line whip" notice and a majority goes against the government in the United Kingdom, that government normally falls and is succeeded by the leading opposition party—or occasionally a coalition—whereas under the American separation of powers into legislative, executive and judicial branches, a legislative defeat for the administration does not bring it down.

It is the duty of the majority and minority legislative whips to round up the members of their respective parties for debates and votes and to attempt to bring doubtful or possibly deviating members into conformity with the party program. The job calls for a great deal of tact, patience, personality—and time. After all, the public has by now been rather thoroughly indoctrinated by commentators and legislators alike with the conviction that most of the actual business of lawmaking is done in committee sessions, and that the floor procedure is mostly window dressing, and so it is. But since the public knows it and the legislator knows it, he sees very little reason to vegetate in his seat during tiresome routine proceedings when he might be at committee meetings or attending to the business of his constituents in his office. So the solons trickle away, to the concern of the whips, and the window dressing rather more resembles the interval between displays—which in fact it is.

A number of means may be resorted to by opponents of legislation to prevent its enactment—or even to forestall any consideration of a bill or resolution. The measure may be "pickled" in committee, or hearings may be tentatively agreed upon and then postponed time after time; the measure may be called up in committee or on the floor (sometimes in the absence of the sponsor) and tabled. There are other ways, as well, but the best-known device is probably the filibuster.

Filibusters are most often associated in the public mind with proceedings in the United States Senate, because Senate rules make it extremely difficult to shut off a speaker by invoking cloture, *i.e.*, limitation of debate, which currently means by a two-thirds vote of those present and voting, a quorum being present. It has been defined as "long-continued speechmaking by a member, or members, of a legislative body, deliberately intended to compel the majority to abandon part of its legislative program." * The definition has its faults, since a filibuster may be, and has been, conducted not alone by lengthy speaking but by resort to enforcement of rules customarily ignored. *e.g.*, compelling the reading at length by the clerk of the journal of the previous day's proceedings or the reading of bills, memorials, or resolutions in full—and more slowly than usual. Nor need the purpose of a filibuster be to compel surrender by a majority. It may be used as a counter tactic against the methods of an obstreperous minority or individual, or it may be used merely to focus widespread public attention upon a particular situation. On most occasions, there are Democrats and Republicans on both sides of major filibusters, although the number from one party may be far less than that from the other. At times, one-man filibusters have been conducted by exceptionally durable Senators.

And since the Senate of the United States is the last forum where one may speak virtually without let, hindrance or reprisal, except at the polls, there are those who conclude that the irritations of an occasional filibuster are cheap at the price.

---

* Smith and Zurcher, *A Dictionary of American Politics,* p. 130.

There are likewise those who contend, by book and page, that there have been good filibusters as well as bad filibusters.

As we have seen, a bill may pass both houses of a legislature and still fail enactment into law. This may occur through a veto by the chief executive. But a bill may come to an ignoble end, even though passed by both houses and not returned to them by the chief executive. This happens when a bill receives a "pocket veto," which results when the President fails to sign a bill within the number of days stipulated by law if, at the end of that time, the legislature is in adjournment. Under such circumstances the bill does not become law.

Where will you find the printed laws? At the end of each session of the state legislatures, the acts of that session are bound into a volume, which can be found in any law library in that state. It is very probable that your state representative or senator can obtain a copy of the most recent session's laws for you, without charge or at nominal cost. It is unlikely he will be able to get older volumes on the same basis.

The public laws of the United States Congress are also bound annually, but copies are not made available to members of Congress for general distribution. Of course, these also may be found in most law libraries and in any large library. Your congressman can always procure for you gratis individual copies of recently enacted public laws and may be able to obtain those for several years back if the printed supply has not been exhausted.

Each member of Congress also has available to him for distribution a small number of extra subscriptions to the daily Congressional Record. If his allotment has not been used, he may add your name to the subscription list; if there are no vacancies, he will probably be glad to add you to his list to be sent a subscription when a vacancy occurs in his allotted list. Unless you have a real reason for receiving the Congressional

Record, do not be unwary enough to become a subscriber. Unless you look them over shortly after they arrive, they will accumulate on you without mercy, like the rising water in *The Sorcerer's Apprentice,* and you will go down under a flood of printed matter.

Also, they are expensive to print and deliver—it is your own money you're spending. Also, again—nine out of every ten pages are as dull as dishwater!

12. "We Wuz Robbed!"

THERE are some rotten apples in every barrel. In every community there are those who know the shady tricks by which elections may be stolen. They will use them if the incentive exists—and the opportunity. A crooked politician may more than cancel out, by vote thievery, the most diligent efforts of the honest political worker. Elections won in the ballot box are sometimes lost in the tabulations, due to the inexperience or neglect of the opposition watchers or committeemen or to the failure to have polls manned by party workers.

Vote frauds may be prevented. The answer lies in alertness by political workers before the election and at the polls.

To eliminate fraud and to be sure that ineligible voters are not registered or permitted to vote, election workers must know the election laws and the tricks used by the unscrupulous to circumvent the laws.

The first step is to be certain that the voting lists (or street lists, as they are sometimes called) are "clean," *i.e.*, that they are free of fraudulent or ineligible registrants.

Precincts or entire elections may be lost because floaters (i.e., transients) or other ineligible voters were allowed to vote. The alert party worker will see that this does not happen in his bailiwick.

What precautions may be taken against fraudulent registrations? *

---

* Acknowledgment is made here for material appearing in this chapter to Democratic and Republican official releases and to *Republican Precinct Workers Handbook,* by J. L. East, National Precinct Workers Publishers Inc. (1946)

Consult your state registration laws. Most states provide a deadline for completion of registration in advance of election day. Provision is usually made for publication of voting or street lists. Check these for suspicious indications of padding. Are an unusually large number of people listed as living in a house or apartment, more than there would seem to be room for? If so, investigate. Your suspicions may be confirmed. You may discover even more floaters in rooming houses and hotels.

Some states require proprietors of hotels, apartments, and rooming houses to supply the election board with lodging-house affidavits. These may have been padded with nonresidents through collusion with a political worker and the proprietor or clerk of the lodging house. Examine these affidavits: does there seem to be a family relationship in the apartment or suite? Does it appear that Mr. Smith has been endowed with a non-existent Mrs. Smith by the addition of her name before or after the execution of the affidavit? You can often get the information from employees or other residents of the lodging house. If you have not checked your lists, you will not be in a position to challenge ineligible voters at the polls.

You may also be able to check your voting lists by telephone calls or registered mail letters, "Return Receipt Requested," if you are prevented from making personal calls by the proprietor or if personal calls would excite suspicion or hostility.

Having located your ineligible or fraudulently registered voters, you may file a petition with the court or registration commission to strike such names from the voting lists (the lawyers for your ward or city or county committee will do this for you) or you may challenge the right of such a person to vote when he appears at the polls. If time permits, the strike-off petition is the better method since argument, if any, will then occur before election day. Valuable time will not be lost in controversy at the polling place. It is significant that thousands of names are stricken from voting lists.

Some vote-catching methods fall short of fraud but can do your party just as much damage if the party worker is not alert to forestall them. Under this head comes the use of false and misleading arguments; for example, the committeemen who plead tearfully that their job is at stake in this particular election. The voter may be led through sympathy to vote against his convictions by such a plea. Voters are sometimes promised business by the committeeman if the voter will go along with the committeeman's ticket. Most of these assurances dissolve into nondelivery after the election, but the vote is in the box. Keep your eyes and ears open for these devices. If you learn of them, try to establish in the voters' minds the misleading character of the arguments given him. Show him that the committeeman may have lost other elections without putting his job in jeopardy, that promises to deliver business are another way of buying votes. You may not win all of your arguments but you should be able to counteract some of the efforts of your opposition.

Among the most contemptible vote-stealing devices is the last-minute anonymous circular containing false attacks upon candidates, circulated too late for repudiation and exposure. This is often found to have originated with radical, fanatic or unscrupulous groups, who have for the time being hitched their kite to the cause of a candidate or political party. There is little direct defense against them except by pointing out to the voter who may have received such a circular how little to be relied on are scurrilous statements to which no one dares sign his name. If their origin can be determined later and prosecution instituted against the persons responsible, there would be less likelihood of a recurrence. Unfortunately, there is generally a disposition after election to forget the whole thing.

A similar filthy device is the vile, inflammatory, and indefensible last-minute circular known as a "roorback" or "Roarback," first used against the presidential candidate, James K. Polk, in 1844. This is an appeal, supposedly signed by supporters of Party A, directed to Catholics, for example, urging the election of a Protestant because there are said to be too many Catholics in office. The Protestants in the same area also receive an appeal, similarly purporting to be signed by supporters of party A, urging the election of a Catholic on the grounds that there are too many Protestants in office. The intention of course is that the voter will believe that the inflammatory literature was intended for voters of a different faith and that an appeal is being made to prejudice, by Party A, against his religious faith. Needless to say, the circulars were distributed by someone interested in the success of Party B. What has been said above about the desirability of bringing to justice the perpetrators of these malicious schemes is even more applicable here.

In the voting place on election day the party worker finds the greatest need for alertness and for vigilant assistance from his colleagues. Here are some of the things to watch for:

Failure to initial ballots (where required). In some states any mark upon the ballot other than the voter's cross marks or checks voids the ballot. In other states, the judge of election is required to initial the voter's ballot, otherwise it is void. If the election official is not to be trusted, he may hand a ballot to one of the voters of your party and appear to initial it, while actually no mark is made. *If your state laws require initialing*, watch carefully to see that the ballots of your voters are properly initialed to comply with the law. And the time to protest a violation is when it occurs. Do not wait.

Chain voting. Where election officials are cheating, chain voting may be worked in several ways. A voter receiving a ballot enters the voting booth and on his return drops what looks like a ballot in the box. He retains the actual ballot and gives it to a party worker outside the polls, who then marks it for his party or candidates. It is handed to the next controlled voter who drops it into the ballot box and returns his own unused ballot for marking outside and use by the next controlled voter. The same scheme may be worked by giving the first voter two ballots, one to be cast, the other to be delivered outside and marked for the next voter. Or marked ballots for one party may be concealed by an election official, and when a voter of another party, instead of dropping his ballot into the box as he should, hands his ballot to the official, the official drops the previously marked ballot in the box, palming the opposition ballot.

Manipulating voting machines. Voting machines are not infallible. Study the instructions which accompany the machine. Election crooks may manipulate them mechanically, if not being watched, by ringing up a number of votes for their party in advance while apparently testing and setting up the machine. They may then similarly manipulate the tallies of votes if they have others in the polling place working with them. Be certain that all cylinders in the machine are set at zero when the polls open and that no unauthorized persons touch the voting mechanism of the machine for any purpose. Check the voting lists of votes cast with the counter on the machine from time to time. The counter can be seen without touching the machine. If there is a model of the machine, use the model to instruct voters who are unfamiliar with or hesitant about voting on the machine. Provision is usually made for instruction of election officials and voters in the use of voting machines in advance of elections.

Illegal assistance. This is certainly one of the most widely practiced of all vote frauds. The law in many states provides that a voter who is unable through physical incapacity or illiteracy to cast his vote unaided may receive assistance. The law usually designates by whom the assistance may be rendered, *i.e.,* whether by election officials only or by members of the voter's party. It is remarkable how many voters request assistance because they have left their glasses at home or broken

150

them the day before, or because of an injured arm or some similarly claimed disability. This type of forgetfulness or casualty appears to be epidemic or at least may occur constantly in one precinct while across the street in another precinct similar symptoms occur with much less frequency. Perhaps the alertness of the opposition has something to do with it. The law is explicit on when assistance may be rendered, how, and by whom. It should be strictly complied with.

Marked ballots. Ballots may be illegally marked in many ways. There are so many that an illustration will have to suffice. Have you ever heard of the pencil-lead trick? The laws of most states provide that a ballot marked in any but the prescribed manner is void. An unscrupulous ballot stealer inserts under his fingernail a small piece of pencil lead. While apparently counting or sorting the paper ballots, he uses the lead to mark opposition ballots illegally. Or he may detect ballots that were inadvertently left blank. In goes an X for his party or candidate. He may also spoil ballots by affixing illegal marks.

Getting workers away from the polls. Obviously, a certain amount of privacy is beneficial to the election crook. So it will help him if he can get the workers of the opposition party away from the polls, if only for a little while. The skilled vote thief doesn't need much time. So, keep your polls manned at all times during the voting and the counting. If you must be away, leave at least one reliable worker in your place. Avoid getting into arguments that may be started to divert your attention from some skullduggery or to get you out of the polling place or involved in an altercation that may land you in court during the valuable voting hours. Look out for the friendly enemy who assures you that it will be all right for you to leave for a while, that he will look after everything while you are gone. That is just what he may do—with your voters as well as his. Do not leave the polling place unwatched until the voting is ended, the counting finished, and the records sealed for delivery to the central place designated for their receipt. Better check on the actual delivery, too.

Voting absentees and tombstones. If the voting lists are not being carefully checked at the polls, floaters may be brought in and voted in substitution for absentees or because their own names are illegally on the list. Or votes may be cast on the voting machine or paper ballots in the names of ineligible voters, without anyone actually appearing in their names at the polls. Obviously, this is the more easily done if no one is checking.

Deliberate stalling. In some precincts, the opposition may have brought out the major part of its voters before the last hour or two of the voting day. If, during those closing hours, the major number of voters are believed to be favorable to your party, your opponents may resort to delaying tactics to slow up the voting and lengthen the line of those waiting their turn. Watch for signs of such a slowdown and be prepared to protest it vigorously. The more voters who hear you the better. They will know that you are battling to get them into the polls; since you are saving their time, many of them will approve. Also, you are lessening the possibility that some will grow weary of waiting and go home without voting, for you have relieved the tedium of the wait; you have made something interesting happen. If the slowdown continues, take down the names of all the parties taking part in it, note the names of witnesses and lodge a complaint with the judge of election. And, if there is time, telephone your complaint in to the election board or to one of the legal advisers of your party.

Buying votes. The not too uncommon method of stealing elections by paying for votes with cash or drinks is apt to occur out of sight of the polling place. But if you are sufficiently alert, you can probably detect it. If this is happening in more than a ew scattered instances, the voters looking for a buyer, or the payoff man himself, may become careless and drop some word that will establish what is going on. Frequent whispered conversations with the same man, an insistence on the part of a number of voters on speaking with a particular individual before voting, or an unusual number of requests for assistance in voting may be suspicious circumstances. The presence of an increasing number of drunks around the polls or the passing round of the bottle may also tip you off that everything is not entirely on the up and up. Right here the use of the countermeasure suggested in the next paragraph can be quite effective.

Countermeasure. Many experienced precinct workers find that a little applied psychology helps prevent vote frauds. They carry with them a little notebook. If it is suspected that fraud is afoot or in contemplation, out comes the notebook and entries are made from time to time, accompanied by a discreet amount of ostentation. It matters not a bit what goes in the notebook, whether pothooks or doodles. The entry is the thing. A guilty conscience can be expected to do the rest. The would-be election trickster does not know what is being entered or what use may be made of it. The appearance is that evidence is being preserved, and it makes for his discomfiture, and, perhaps, may assure the ballot's integrity. Sometimes the use of a camera (with or without film) clicking away at suspicious happenings will accomplish the same purpose.

Watch the tally. After the polls close, the tally of the ballots is conducted. The usual procedure is for one of the election officers to call out the results, as read from the paper ballots or machine, to the clerks who tally them. The tally, or written record of votes cast, is usually set down by two or three clerks on separate sheets, and all of these must conform accurately. See that they do. If you are a division committeeman, keep your own tally sheet as well, or have one of your watchers keep it.

153

If the election count does not agree with your tally, insist on a recount. Do not be talked out of it. Any effort to persuade you to desist, such as the plea that it is already very late and everyone is tired, is in itself a suspicous circumstance. Keep in mind that the tally may go wrong either if the election official is calling off incorrect figures or if the tally clerks are entering them incorrectly. Stick with your job until the tally is entirely completed and checked, the returns sealed, and all election law requirements complied with. Then, if you are not too tired, you can go down to the party headquarters and see how your colleagues did.

A final word: *Elections may be stolen from the top as well as from the bottom.*

There were caesars before Caesar—and after him—who dealt in *panen et circensem,* bread and circuses. Caesar, Pontifex Maximus, was high priest not only of the corrupted religion of the day but of a debauched electorate as well. He poured out the public monies from the treasury for their amusement; he manipulated the price of their bread; he told them always that these blessings came from Caesar. And it was quite a while before the Roman people tumbled to the fact that the big party was on them after all.

And Octavian, who came after and became Augustus, set everything to rights after his fashion. "He found Rome brick and left it marble." He found a Rome that had been free; was it his fault, or Caesar's, that Romans had sold out for security and glamour? Or was it the fault of the people?

Overinflated payrolls, printing press money, and government largess for political purposes may corrupt the electorate as surely as vote stealing at the polls, and much more successfully. The American colonists in righteous anger kicked out the British King because he had sent a horde of officeholders to oppress them. But we keep on discovering that eternal vigilance is the price of our liberty. Whenever history repeats itself, we must be

repared to rid ourselves of such hordes of oppressive office-
olders; they prepare the way for Caesar.

Those who seek power beyond the will and intent of the
eople gain their foothold by winning over the voters with ap-
ealing promises; something for nothing, security without work,
ntertainment without price. After all, Mussolini and Hitler
vere elected at "perfectly legal" elections, so far as the electoral
orms were concerned.

As Maxwell Anderson has George Washington say, in *Valley
orge,* "This liberty will look easy by and by when nobody dies
o get it."

13. Shall We Join the Ladies?

"THE information herein contained is not guaranteed, but is obtained from sources that we believe to be reliable," as brokers observe wistfully, on the cover page of their stock offerings.

It could not be otherwise, for it would be a hardy male indeed who would undertake to dogmatize about the role of women in politics. I am glad to take refuge (coward that I am!) in the assurance that the material for this chapter has been culled from information furnished by the ladies themselves.

The information, comments and observations herein are derived from Marjorie, from Hannah, from Sally, Lilias, Elsie June, Louise, Marian, and Barbara, and a host of others. They have furnished wise and incisive and witty contributions. So I give you their own views, not alone because it is safer that way, but in the interest of a more accurate presentation. This is the way they see it. If the author dares to insert an occasional discreet interpretation along the way, he will endeavor to do so in such ways as to avoid detection. Or recrimination.

Shall we join the ladies, then? Or rather, since the ladies have joined us, shall we have a look into coeducational politics?

Eight key questions were submitted to a small group of women who were politically active and informed; all of them had attained eminence as recognized leaders of political groups. To be consulted concerning the views of women in politics is no new experience to any of them. These were the questions asked:

1) Have women raised the general level of politics?
2) Do women make good politicians? Good candidates?

3) As politicians, what are their virtues? Their faults?
4) Are women's political clubs effective? If so, how?
5) Are women in politics more—or less—candid than men?
6) Do you believe women should support special health and welfare legislation for their benefit?
7) Should they support the Equal Rights Amendments?
8) Are they willing to assume a more active share in the policy-making sphere of politics?

Obviously, these particular questions were not intended to be all embracing. It was felt that they might rather be evocative, that other suggestions might be forthcoming as well as specific answers to these inquiries. The answers did bring many other helpful suggestions and comments.

There was general unanimity with regard to the first query. All agreed that women have indeed raised the level of politics, a conclusion in which not all male politicians will concur. Some of the latter point to the continuance of old political evils such as election frauds and mediocre candidates. The ladies reply that there is today more decorum and less fraud at the polling place and that the general caliber of party candidates and the content of party programs are superior to the days before equal suffrage. And the ladies are emphatic in their view that the participation of women in politics is responsible for a more enlightened condition in civic affairs. It is fair to say that majority opinion of voters of both sexes supports the view that the activity of women in politics has brought about real betterment.

As one collaborator says, "Politics, in its true meaning—participation in good government—knows no sex," but she nods with justifiable pride toward the national federations, the state councils, and the local women's political clubs as evidence of alert and effective participation in politics. Another correspondent makes the point that "through such organizations . . . the women have fostered an educational system which keeps the members informed and this education is translated into political activity which has been a material help to the . . . Party."

As to whether women make good politicians, there is little doubt that they do. Some qualifications are heard that bear rather on the question of opportunity than of ability. Those suggesting anything less than unqualified approval of women as politicians are in the minority. The usual reaction is, "Yes, indeed they are!" and with *ad personam* logic, they cite by name many well-known and successful women politicians. "Some of our leaders," says one (who is no small shakes as a leader herself), "are important nationally and on a state level in the policy-making groups. It is interesting to watch them develop their candidates and issues."

As politicians, their principal—and justifiable—complaint is that they are denied equal political opportunity in competition with their male counterparts. Certainly, on the national scene, when presented with equal opportunity, as in the case of Frances Bolton, Clare Boothe Luce, Edith Green, Margaret Chase Smith, Florence Dwyer, Edna Kelly, Charlotte Reid, and Maureen Neuberger, for example, they have asked—and given—no quarter and have acquitted themselves with distinction as constructive builders in the house of government. The same is true in the administration of state and local affairs.

What they think of themselves as politicians, they reflect in estimating women as candidates for political office. Women are as good candidates as men, in about the same proportion, they reply; some feel that women candidates may bring more credit to their party and contribute to it effective and favorable publicity. Virtually none of them concedes that women fall short of male candidates in any particular. One interesting challenge is worth noting: "Can you recall any single instance where women candidates have been involved in political scandal or proven chicanery?"

As politicians and candidates they resent the tendency of the men to compartmentalize them—to hold the major offices for themselves, yielding only a little ground here and there, with the statement that this or that job is of the sort "a woman can hold." They are also critical of the narrowness implicit in such condescending comment as "maybe we ought to find a place for one woman on the ticket." They ask, "Why *one* woman? Don't we cast half, or more, of the votes?" And, aware of the political tendency to give roughly proportionate representation based on geographical or racial or religious grounds, they inquire, are there not as many women as men? Don't they own more than half of the wealth? Nor do they agree that there is any logical limitation on the kind of job a woman can hold. Women in America have held almost every kind of job there is in industry, the professions, and in politics. As they view it, it is no longer a matter of proving the point but of expanding its application.

What assets do women bring to the practice of politics? The ladies, in replying, were more generous in appraisal of their sex than they are sometimes credited with being. Says one, "Forthrightness, intellectual integrity, integrity also of purpose and capacity for unity in action." As all who know this particular correspondent will attest, she herself possesses all of these qualities, together with personal charm and great good looks. In any event, her convictions, as implemented by the performance of her political responsibilities, raise a standard to which others (both male and female) may repair, if General Washington will pardon the paraphrase on his message to the colonists.

Another sums up the virtues of women in politics in this fashion: "Stress on clean elections; given something definite to do are dependable; do not vacillate; are self-sacrificing; their intuition and study of problems, local, state—national and international—make for effective thinking and action." Again the writer must take time out to marvel at the generosity of the other

159

sex, and to wonder whether a similar questionnaire addressed to he-politicians would have elicited any such high evaluation?

An asset that women politicians enumerate is that women are inclined to demand candidates of higher caliber and to insist upon positive programs and policies. To the outside observer, it is fairly obvious that more stress is laid upon this in the political meetings of women than of men; whether these demands are pressed as effectively as they might be is at least an arguable point. But the effectiveness of similar demands from business and labor organizations (where largely attended by men) is arguable too.

One woman, holding a most important political office, states: "Women are more active in seeking information with which to inform the electorate; in giving of themselves and their continuous efforts without seeking compensation; in believing in their party and their candidates and in working for both."

As one approaches (somewhat warily) a consideration of the possible faults or drawbacks of women in the political field, it is striking that one of the qualities just referred to as an asset— the giving of effort without seeking compensation—is condemned by another commentator as a fault. One lady (who has never sought any paid political position for herself) observes that women who engage in political activity commit political error in not demanding political jobs as a reward for their services "as do the men."

In facing up to shortcomings politically (although one woman writes, "cannot think of any!"), most of these experts agree that women are not sufficiently impersonal in their approach to political problems or in their appraisal of candidates. As one woman phrases it, "I would say that perhaps the greatest fault is an overinterest; a tendency to be shortsighted about party faults; a tendency to take the close and not the over-all picture of an election so that immediate things make them either excessively optimistic or deeply pessimistic—all due to a devotion to a cause which may sometimes make virtues of faults."

On the question of the effectiveness of women's political clubs, there appears to be general agreement that they are achieving desired ends. Approval of them is mostly uncritical and enthusiastic. It may well be that a similar question addressed to women uninterested in politics might have brought a different answer. All of the women actually consulted are active in politics and all of them participate in women's political organizations; and they approve of them. One reason generally advanced is that women's political clubs are useful instruments to inspire better political work and that women need this social stimulus in order to work politically.

Let's hear what the leading organizer of these clubs in a large metropolitan area has to say, "I am an incurable optimist about women's political clubs. To be happy in politics, women must be informed and inspired. Women members have a sphere of influence too often underestimated. They are a source of power in their own families, their churches, their nonpolitical organizations, in the grocery lines, over the back fence, and on the telephone. Members are usually strongly partisan. Their meetings give an opportunity to candidates to air policies and issues, and they are a source of constant publicity. They have continuity, functioning always from year to year with at least four meetings a year."

Others comment that women, acting together in political clubs, not only promote better civic awareness through discussion and speechmaking, but bring civic responsibility home to their members by assigning them tasks in practical political work, such as raising money through ingenious fund-raising devices, providing forums for candidates, "pulling" * doorbells, *i.e.,* getting electors registered and into the polling places.

---

* *i.e.,* ringing doorbells. A political archaism still much used by precinct workers, harking back to Victorian door pulls.

Since women possess a greater part of the wealth in this country than do men, it is remarkable that politicians were so short-sighted for so long in not availing themselves of womanpower in fund-raising. The excuse was that the amount raised wouldn't justify the effort or that women would solicit and accept contributions from large contributors in amounts less than the men would get from them, thus "ruining" the contributor for an effective touch.

Here I have some pride as an innovator in that, being responsible for a national political fund-raising campaign some years ago, I reversed previous custom, overrode the customary objections and turned over a substantial part of the job to the national women's party organization. The results were good and have been increasingly more effective. The old fears and inhibitions proved to be groundless.

Men in politics today do not, as a rule, underestimate the value and importance of women's political organizations. Certainly, they should not. Some male politicians profess to scoff at them as useless gossip groups, but one feels that their heart isn't in it. If they have had any experience at all, they must have learned that it is better to have the women on their side. In fact, men seem to be more aware of the political power of women than are the women themselves. If it were not so, women would not have labored so long in the political vineyard with so small a proportion of the fruits of political activity. The ladies may be right in their estimate that their sex is more willing to work without compensation. That is true in the household, too. But many women receiving compensation for their efforts appear to favor such an arrangement.

It is safe to say that during the average political campaign a candidate speaks more often to women's organizations than to men's groups. Women do seem to be more interested in seeing for themselves what the candidate looks like and what he talks like and what sort of a wife he has. A candidate usually reasons that women are more likely to vote for him if he has made a personal appearance before them (assuming that he makes a favorable impression), whereas it is thought that men may often be satisfied with the fact that the candidate is running on a particular ticket, or that they like what they have read about him and his views. Candidates also know that they are more likely to be asked direct, candid, and at times embarrassing questions by an audience of women. Even so, most candidates make it a point to attend as many meetings of women's organizations as they can. This in itself would seem to furnish further evidence of the importance of women's political organizations.

As to whether women in politics are more—or less—candid than men, the ladies have no doubts whatever. The answers all run the same way. Women, they assert with one voice, are so much more candid than men that there is no room for comparison. One feels that those replying wonder why the question was asked.

The question "do you believe women should support special health and welfare legislation for their benefit?" proved to have been incautiously worded. The questioner was promptly brought to book. A majority of those answering put their finger on the fly in the ointment. Not health and welfare legislation for their benefit alone, they protested. Women should support such legislation for the benefit of *all* citizens.

"Support of health and welfare legislation generally," said one, "results in healthy community growth and good family relationships. Such support is not selfish because it is for the good of the family and that includes the men as well as the women in the community."

Women, they emphasize, should be all out for legislation, such as equal pay for equal work, child care, prevention of juvenile delinquency, maternity benefits, care for dependent children, social security, better education, better housing. They recognize room for legislative improvement at all governmental levels.

Women do and have supported special health and welfare legislation in the interest of all of the people of the community. This has been an outstanding contribution of women in politics, they aver. "The legislative committees of the women's political groups function better than any other committee; their liberal ideals have led the way for many years in legislative bodies."

One point they might have made had they not presumably deemed it to be self-evident: The major advances in progressive health and welfare enactments date, for the most part, from a period not long after the adoption of universal suffrage.

Should women in politics support equal rights legislation? This turned out to be the sixty-four dollar question. Answers ranged from "yes" to "no" by way of "they should continue to study the proposals to ascertain if this is the most effective method of eliminating unnecessary inequalities." (!)

Among those favoring equal rights legislation, the argument runs that women have proven themselves competitively in peacetime pursuits, and in our wars women have worked with men from the assembly line to the front line. Women are often distressed by restrictive laws that hamper their economic and legal status. Even the more liberal state laws limit the rights of women in industry, and the woman wage earner still has some legal handicaps especially at state levels.

Opponents counter that laws must continue to be enacted that will be fair to women and regardful of their needs, but mere "equality" is not fairness. Enactment of equal rights laws will, they contend, erase from the statute books all legislation protecting women in industry, all present safeguards concerning their marital, testamentary, or contractual status. The question of male airline "stewardesses" presents an interesting twist.

Men, one woman points out, must give more recognition to financial contributions by women to political parties. Political organizations cannot exist without financial support and the broader the base of that support the better for the vitality of the party. The administrators of party policy cannot ignore the views of those who make possible its functioning as an effective unit. This is another way of saying that those who help, advise. Many men contribute to a political party, as a matter of course or of custom or (regrettably) of expediency. It ought to be generally understood by women, even by many women politicians, that their participation in the policy-making activities of the party of their choice should increase in proportion as their assistance to the party finances improves, and they should insist upon it.

The more women—and the more men—who share in furnishing the sinews of political war the less the likelihood of domination of the party by a very few, whose willingness to fight the battle through lean days and good has given them increasing reason to expect that their advice will be heeded. Many of a political party's heaviest contributors themselves wish that there were thousands who would rally to the support of the party's financial requirements. In the long view they know that this will be a healthy development. The same interest in party advancement that led them to support it also leads them to desire that this support shall be shared by those of like views and affiliations.

One woman submits this query, "Are women willing to assume the responsibility of policy making or do they prefer to carry out the plans formulated by the men leaders?" Another answers, "They are not only willing but eager, but they are not given the opportunity by the men." Again, they should insist upon a larger hand in policy decisions.

In most localities, women, after forty years of active participation and doorbell pulling, are not sitting in at the early stages before primaries to help choose candidates. They are not as a rule sitting in at meetings of party leaders before legislative sessions to aid in shaping policies. Who is to blame? The women? The men leaders?

This is not to say that women political leaders are never consulted. They are, but most of them know that they are not called into the inner councils as a matter of course. The usual procedure is to confer separately with one or more women who are asked to express "the woman's point of view" on specific legislation or to indicate which of a list of candidates may or may not be acceptable to women voters and, too often, after the decisions have been, at least tacitly, arrived at. In the opinion of many women leaders, there are not enough instances where even this degree of consultation is solicited. Who is to blame? As elsewhere indicated, it is possible that male politicians are more aware than women of the political power of women voters. This would suggest that women are backward in demanding a greater place in party councils or, perhaps, that they prefer to have policy made by the male politicians. Yet, they deny the latter assumption. Taking this denial at face value, then the women themselves have somehow missed the boat in securing policy-making influence for themselves.

It has already been postulated that they have missed the boat in the important particular of rising to authority through the fact of their increased sharing in political-party financing. Granted that many women cannot afford to contribute, yet those who can, according to their means, are not doing so in nearly the same proportion as men in comparable financial condition. But this single default is clearly not the whole story.

Part of the answer may lie in one of the shortcomings referred to by the women themselves, that is failure to insist on recognition proportionate to the political gains resulting from their efforts, not merely willingness to work without financial compensation. Men in politics often do that too; their participation may have meant personal sacrifice or financial loss. But the average male politico so situated is likely to do his best to heighten his political stature by bringing his accomplishments to the attention of those party leaders in a position to enlarge his sphere of political participation or influence.

Can it be that women in politics miss out on the "follow through" by regarding activity in political clubs and at the polls as an end in itself rather than as a means to a larger goal? It is not the meeting that is important, it is what is done as a result of the meeting. It is not alone victory at the polls but what is done with the victory.

If the victory has been won in substantial part by the skillful work of women politically active, have not the women a duty to follow through with participation in the legislative program of the party which they helped to send to the Capitol? If they are waiting for an invitation (as Mr. Citizen sometimes waits for an invitation to use his franchise), its extension may continue to be dilatory. Perhaps the woman political worker in the ranks is partly at fault in not urging upon her women leaders insistence upon greater participation in party councils. Perhaps the women leaders should be more insistent on their own hook. Possibly a rereading of the parable of the buried talent is in order.

At which point in this discussion a woman leader can be heard to say, "What about the men leaders? Haven't we earned the right to more recognition?" Of course the men leaders are at fault, too. Their allies have been the *status quo* and inertia. Women earned the right to universal suffrage, but they didn't get it until they fought for it, and what woman has such a paragon of a husband as to have received all the recognition she has earned, without some hinting, and perhaps a bit of aggression now and then on her part?

It is possible that part of the difficulty is strategic. Policy-making takes place at the top levels in any party organization, be it local, state, or national. Policy makers usually stand together. To be accepted in such a group, it must be made apparent to them that the participation of women leaders is desirable, in their interest, in the interest of the party. This means that women will have to help each other upward to such posts. They will have to get together a cheering section for the leaders of their choice and demand recognition for them.

Men usually hold the opinion that women will not stick together, that they will not back each other up, that they will not fight for each other, that they will not vote for women candidates. If this notion is cockeyed, the women will have to be the ones to disabuse the men. And that is where the strategy comes in. If women can make a living pyramid of themselves, if they can agree which among them is to be hoisted to the top of the pile, they will be able to elevate their choices to the policy-making levels.

Politically conscious women deplore male reluctance to extend to them full partnership and equal participation in political goings on. They complain that equality is denied them in organization and administration of political affairs and in the appointment and election of candidates to public office, and that this attitude is unrealistic and arbitrary.

They have accepted, perforce, the halfway approach of co-chairmanships for women and the designation of women leaders as cocommitteemen in political organizations. Their mental reservations persist; these limited and grudging concessions are put, by some women, in the same class with the ghettoing of their sex into separate women's political organizations. Not all women agree. Many of them aver that it is natural and preferable that their political work be concentrated on organizations of their own.

Some progress may be noted. Women occasionally serve as state chairmen of their political party and, in my State, there are five women county chairmen of one party, several of the other and a number of women are now ward leaders in the cities.

But the points of view converge toward unanimity when the question of recognition for service performed is under discussion.

Nearly all interested women appear to be in agreement that the selection of women for political honors is governed by some sort of quota system, and that the quota is grossly inadequate. Men reply that this is due, in part, to the fact that women have come into the political field more recently—but the argument that "we were here first" carries little persuasive force. Ask the American Indian. A more obvious explanation appears to lie in the fact that it is the men who are handing out the honors. Politically ambitious women concede that this kind of governance may be *de facto* but they do not recognize it as *de jure*. The more women attain to the policy-making levels by methods heretofore referred to—and by such other methods as their ingenuity may suggest—the greater will be their share of political recognition.

For a change is coming. Men who would deny it are less wise than King Canute. As the waves ignored the royal command and swept around the throne, so the ex-Waves and the ex-Wacs and the throng of talented women, who have demonstrated under wartime and peacetime conditions that the limitations of sex are few indeed, will not be denied. As any life insurance company will tell you, women by virtue of being the more durable sex, living longer on the average than the brittle male, now hold much more than half of the country's wealth. As taxpayers they intend to obtain that which, as women, has been withheld: full political recognition. Furthermore, their interest in the application of practical politics is waxing as the abrasion on the pocketbook nerve is increasingly felt.

As evidence that the present imbalance between men and women is steadily lessening, it is important to remember that public acceptance of women in public office is steadily growing. The public is getting used to them. Women as state and federal officeholders have acquitted themselves well, in the view of the electorate in general and their numbers are notably on the increase. There has been considerable criticism of the practice of endorsing for elective office the widow of a deceased office-

169

holder in order to capitalize on the good will generated by her husband, to gain the sympathy vote, or to forestall a general contest for the office, just as they might object if the candidate were a son or a brother of the incumbent. Some, but decidedly not all, of the widows have proven as inadequate as many male officeholders, yet it is certainly true that in most cases the circumstances leading to their selection have indicated little consideration of their ability or aptitude. Deserving women possessing proper qualifications for the office are justified in objecting to the choice of a woman because she is a widow. They have logic on their side in arguing that the candidacy of the woman or of a man should be based upon ability to do the job. As a footnote, it ought to be mentioned that many widows, serving in Congress and in state offices, have shed added luster on the family name and in some cases have far exceeded their husbands in substantial contributions to the public service. Others have carried on in their husband's footsteps with about the same measure of competence formerly exhibited by the male partner. Many of them have been reelected again and again on their own merits and, with seniority, have gained strong influence.

Speaking of widows in politics, it may not be amiss to mention that a good many women have become politically active by reason of the development of the careers of their husbands as public officials. Aside from the advantages (and possible disadvantages!) that accrue to the male politician in having a politically alert wife, the lady herself discovers an adventure in helping to turn the civic wheel. Some have chosen political careers for themselves, and some have contented themselves with advancing the careers of their husbands. But they have been, and are, potent factors in the political life of the nation. No asset can be more valuable to a male candidate than a personable and helpful wife.

What of women as constituents of public officials? Any generalizing here hardly seems called for, so far as my own experience goes. Women as constituents seem to react in much the same fashion as do men constituents. They write letters or interview their representatives about the things they want for the community or for themselves; they adopt resolutions; they write letters to the editor; they point with pride or view with alarm; they too forget to vote. They do seem to be somewhat more direct in the expression of their views and more disposed to demand satisfactory answers. They appear to be a bit more persistent in demanding solutions of problems personal to them. They have a long memory about evasive replies or unanswered letters. To the extent that there is deviation between men and women as constituents, it appears to lie in the character of the matters that interest them. Women generally show more interest in matters affecting welfare, public health, the family; the men more in legislation affecting business and labor problems. The difference, however, is one of degree; there is no fundamental cleavage.

Formerly, men appeared to take more interest in foreign affairs than women. The incidences of two disastrous world wars, and our later "undeclared" wars with their tragic impact on family life and the vigorous educational campaigns carried on by women's organizations to emphasize the importance to the individual of personal support of measures for the preservation of world peace and understanding have brought a change. To-day, the interest of women in foreign affairs is about equal to the interest displayed by the men. Which is not to say that the percentage of either men or women actually conferring with their representatives on foreign policy is very great, nor is the public very well informed on the implications of day-to-day developments in external relations. There is much room for improvement in that area. Perhaps their representatives are also at fault in not conveying more information or more candid revelations to their constituents as to the implications of events.

It may not be important that women's organizations seem to have more officers and more committees than one usually finds in the men's organizations. This effort to give every member a title may have some connection with the way women have been treated by the men in politics; it may be an attempt to compensate for the fact that in the competition with men for political recognition they have not been given enough places. Or it may simply be a shrewd realization that the individual will cooperate better if assigned a definite job to do and a title to go with it.

To the he-politician, attending his first meeting of a women's political club, it is an awesome thing to be confronted (before he is called upon for a few words) with the roll call of the reports of officers and committees. After Madam President, there are the First, Second, Third, etc. Vice Presidents, the Recording Secretary, the Corresponding Secretary, the Treasurer, the Assistant Treasurer, the Historian, the Chairman of the Executive Committee, Entertainment Committee, Membership Committee, Memorials Committee, Delinquent Dues Committee, Welfare Committee, Legislative Committee, Convention Committee, and the Special Committee on the Selection of a Gift for our Retiring President, Mrs. Jones.

Some women complain that, in spite of all these deafening reports from the numerous big guns, very few hits are registered on target and not a great deal gets done. Others retort that it is the same way with the men's organizations. These defenders of the existing order argue reasonably that it is quite impossible to maintain interest in political activity throughout the year and that it is better to build up to a peak and to press for effective action as polling time nears. They say that the urge toward gregariousness is satisfied by the meeting together, by the socializing, the discussion of the reports, and the general feeling that the organization is alive and ready to get under way at the proper time.

I submit that the gregarious would find many more women with whom to be gregarious if political women's groups held at least some of their meetings at a time convenient for attendance by working girls and women. I am aware that it is not unusual for meetings to be set for luncheon or dinner hours. But the working part of a three or four hour luncheon meeting comes so late in the proceedings that working girls cannot stay for it. The 4:00 PM tea gatherings may be attended ordinarily by Mrs. Dentist, Mrs. Doctor or Mrs. Lawyer. But the timing rules out Miss Dean of Girls, Miss Teacher, Miss Secretary or Miss Technician. Our greater affluence permits these leisured meetings, one supposes, but one does not find there a spectrum broad enough to include many urban wives or Negroes or persons of slender means, no matter how lively their political interest.

I may add, from the selfish aspect of the male politico, that many women chairmen, unlike their male counterparts, tend to insist that the speaker remain throughout the entire proceedings. This is at the cost of other work the candidate, for example, might be doing during part of those three or four hours he spends wriggling at the table or on the platform.

There is the other side of the shield, where reflection puts the women in the better light. They are definitely more broad-minded than men in their choice of speakers. Not only do they invite men to speak to them—and how many men's organizations list women as the guest speaker of the day?—but their speakers are likely to cover a wider range ideologically. Not all of them are selected because their audience expects them to be in agreement with its general views, as so often happens in male political meetings. Nor are the ladies as apt to confine themselves to speakers on purely political topics. The subject may be exploration, gardening, art, music, travel, or politics. Women are notably more patient than men, and they show it when entrapped by the lengthy rhetoric of a speaker without terminal facilities. Hastily I interject here the fond hope I am not speaking from personal experience! Be it said furthermore in their favor, along with their numerous committee activities, they tend to encourage political discussion groups, round table talks and forums, and they lay greater stress on actually getting their candidates within sight, hearing and question prodding prior to elections.

It has been my observation, with respect to those organizations that are nonpolitical, that the male organizations are quite cautious about inviting candidates to appear before them in advance of an election for fear that the club's officers may be accused of engaging in "politics". In contrast the women's clubs invite a candidate whenever it occurs to them for the good and simple reason that they want to see what he looks like.

As to political organizations generally, I am sure attendance would be better if the proceedings were lightened up with the inclusion of more entertainment and less speeches. I like some skits and some satire. Politics *can* be fun.

Perhaps we may conclude with this thought: Women in politics may find it necessary to remind the men that when a lady enters the room she does not like to remain standing. It might be advisable to offer her a seat.

And a plush one, at that.

14. Then You'll Remember Me

In the United States—and the United Kingdom—political parties parade their orators, depend upon their workhorses, flatter their fund raisers and exploit their window dressers.

To those who keep current with their politics, to define them is to recognize them. But there are others. These extroverts, offbeat, flamboyant, are not of any party or period. They are, of themselves, a breed apart.

True, some anonymous cynic once said, "It's not like the good old days—and it never was." Be that as it may, there does seem to be more sobriety in politics today than in the riotous era of "Pitchfork Ben" Tillman of South Carolina and "Sockless Jerry" Simpson of Texas. The pallid technique of Chicago's Mayor Daley is dull as dishwater compared to the lurid effronteries of "Hinkey Dink" and "Bath House John," now gone to whatever heaven is reserved for politicians of Chicago's gamy past.

Cartoonists to the contrary notwithstanding, the day of the statesman's Prince Albert, black hat and string tie is done. The modern practitioner of civic relations or politics dresses nowadays about the same as any other citizen, perhaps more conservatively than most. Losing himself modestly in conformity with the norm, he is inclined to agree with Alexander Pope's, "Be not the first by whom the new is tried, nor yet the last to lay the old aside." There must be a reason for this. Possibly it resides in the belief that one who looks as much as possible like everyone else may be presumed to think the common thought, to act as his neighbor would act. Certainly, discretion in dress as in speech gives the neighbors less to gossip about.

Fortunately for the public, and for the political reporters, there are still some individualists left. Their distinction of appearance or mannerism is not accidental. They know how the eye roves quickly past the familiar and comes to rest upon the unexpected. They are well aware that their memory may be kept more green among their constituents by discussion of the unruly cowlick or of the fresh blue flower never missing from the buttonhole. Could it be that the great Lincoln's overly tall stovepipe hat was first acquired with such a thought in mind? Certainly his beard was.

True, the flowing mane of James K. Vardaman of Mississippi and the pink whiskers of Jim Ham. Lewis of Illinois remain only in reminiscent memory. The last full beard was lost to the Congress of the United States when Congressman Tinkham stormed back to Massachusetts in 1944. The Vardaman shoulder-length bob recalls an anecdote. In a primary battle between Vardaman and the brilliant John Sharp Williams for the same Senate seat, there were those who called it "a contest between hair and brains."

Members of the present Congress, when in the gallery showing visiting firemen the best known public figures on the House floor, are wont to point out not merely the Speaker and the majority and minority leaders. The identifying finger singles out the member whose suit is made without pockets, the member whose curly hair is cut so that it is never parted, the member wearing the artist's flowing black tie or the white "ice cream suit." If the constituents have been sufficiently bemused, perhaps one of them will pick up the check at the ensuing luncheon in the House restaurant.

Individual characteristics that have brought fame or notoriety to public officials are not confined to either side of the water.

176

One thinks of the ill-fated Chamberlain's umbrella, of the white tie of Laval, he of evil soul. On the bright side, are the Churchill hats and ever present cigar, and Field Marshal Montgomery's beret, or Roosevelt's long cigarette holder, Senator Bobby Kennedy's bushy mop, and Lyndon Johnson's big Texas hat.

Some public figures have given the public memory a helpful nudge by insisting upon the use of their nicknames on every occasion. Among tabs that come to mind (thanks partly to their authors!) are Senator "Pappy" O'Daniel of Texas, Governor "Pa" and Governor "Ma" Ferguson of that same eminent domain. Representatives "Pat" Kearney of New York, "Took" Gathings of Arkansas, "Runt" Bishop of Illinois. And was it only in New York that people knew Fiorello LaGuardia as their "Little Flower"?

How do the members of the state and federal legislatures get along with each other? Generally speaking very well indeed. The spirit of live and let live is highly developed. In spite of heated and vigorous exchanges in debate on the floor, the members ordinarily preserve friendly feelings toward each other, irrespective of party lines. Many of them are lawyers, accustomed to strenuous advocacy in the courtroom and to the brotherhood of the bar outside. But lawyers, farmers, journalists, businessmen, they are all engaged as legislators in the art of persuasion. And those who oppose one day may be allies in another cause on the next.

This tradition of fair dealing, of sportsmanship, of respect for the convictions of others, is one of the best features of our political way of life. It goes a long way to explain why our system has stood the parliamentary strain while other governments have gone down in riot and revolution.

An illustration comes to mind: After a particularly fierce interchange on the floor of one legislative body between the recognized leader of the extreme left wing and an outstanding spokesman for the strongly conservative position, the two men met in the lobby. Said one, "I'll make you a proposition; take me up and we will both be sure to be reelected." "What's on your mind?" said the other. "Why, it's simple; you just speak *against me* out in my district and I'll do the same for you in yours!"

The custom of fair play expresses itself in many ways. A legislator, about to launch an attack upon the position of another member during debate, will generally advise his opponent of the time he intends to speak so that his adversary may have an opportunity to be present and to defend himself if he so desires. An occasional failure to abide by this ethical understanding can result in lasting bitterness.

Legislators of the same party will often rally round a colleague in distress who is anticipating criticism at home or who faces a difficult fight for reelection. Laudatory speeches will be made about him and the record he has made in the legislature. Be sure the build-up is appreciated, and reciprocated.

What are some pet legislative aversions? Well, very few of them like the member who is perpetually demanding roll calls or quorum calls. These require the interruption of necessary office business and work for, or interviews with, constituents. They also put other members in a bad light if they are absent too often. The solon with a sovereign remedy for every single public ill is a bit of a headache also. So are the legislative nit-pickers.

Another legislative itch is the "popper-upper," the member who is always jumping to his feet with half-baked observations or ill-considered objections. And none too popular are the constituents who demand unreasonable personal services, or those who force the weary member to come up with the same old dog-eared answers to such questions as, "What's it like up at the Capitol? A madhouse, I'll bet!"

One type of legislator who unerringly provokes wrath is the character who, by book and page, revels in exposing the inconsistencies of his fellows. For if there is one thing concerning which public officials are especially sensitive, it is to be baldly confronted with an apparent inconsistency. The defense to such an attack has come almost to assume a pattern. The affronted one is quite likely to enter the fray, often with wordy dignity, but nearly always armed with two allusions. In the first place, he will say, consistency may be said by some to be a jewel, but in this instance it is but a semiprecious stone, and I will tell you why, etc. And (as a triumphant riposte) in the second place, remember that as Emerson so well put it, "A foolish consistency is the hobgoblin of little minds."

Speaking of favorite quotations heard in legislative halls, there are some that recur again and again. The favorites are from Jefferson and Lincoln, or from Washington's Second Inaugural or from his Farewell Address. Alexander Hamilton is currently "out," but he may come into fashion again. Daniel Webster also seems to be out of fashion, but not quite as much as Henry Clay. Edmund Burke, 18th Century Man of Parliament, is a hardy perennial.

There are some unfailing stand-bys, Henley's "Invictus" ("I am the captain of my soul") and almost anything from Edgar Guest, as for example, "Somebody said that it couldn't be done, but he with a laugh replied, that maybe it couldn't but he wouldn't be one to say so until he had tried." Another is that inspirational piece about the high soul on the high road, and the low soul on the low, in which the speaker somehow becomes associated with the high soul. Among political essayists, the not entirely optimistic commentary of Alexis de Tocqueville is freely drawn upon.

Far and away the favorite of the longer poetic quotes is this, from "The Day's Demand" by Josiah Gilbert Holland:

God give us men! A time like this demands
  Strong minds, great hearts, true faith, and ready hands;
Men whom the lust of office does not kill;
  Men who possess opinions and a will;
Men who have honor; men who will not lie;
  Men who can stand before a demagogue
And damn his treacherous flatteries without winking;
  Tall men, sun-crowned, who live above the fog
In public duty and in private thinking.

I pray that you will not mistake candor for condemnation. You will have noticed that, while not all of the favorite allusions of men in positions of responsibility are great poetry, they have a common denominator: they evidence a respect for certain eternal verities. Legislators are very busy people and there is not much time for scholarly research, even where the capacity for it exists. Nor does it follow that more profound allusions would be more effective. These virtues—love of freedom, integrity, courage, determination—may be but imperfectly realized, but the fact remains that they are aspired to.

Before you heave that first stone, is there much glass in your house?

15. May You Fare Well

IF you have stayed the course of this discussion, you will have gathered something of how to make a beginning in the world of politics, of how interest may become participation and how participation promotes progress either as worker, candidate or public official.

You have taken part, as reader, in an examination of what qualities the political animal should have and of some steps to be trod as well as missteps to be shunned.

We have examined the nature of public opinion and of its sometime source, public relations.

Some questions have been posed and answers proffered. The discussion of how to campaign for office has been included upon the assumption that anyone, man or woman, becoming genuinely involved in the political current, will be interested in what happens during electoral contests, whether one's interest is in the passive role of observer, the activist task of political worker or the exciting challenges of candidacy.

Since the majority of electoral campaigns at the national and state level are for legislative seats, it has been deemed useful to discuss in this book how we, the people, come by the laws we must live by. This has necessitated an examination of what leads legislators to introduce or to support legislative proposals and to examine the process by which these may evolve into laws for the regulation of personal or corporate conduct.

In keeping pace with the onflowing political stream, illustrations by reference to personalities may become dated. As events change, new techniques are devised to cope with them. These changes, in a time of rapidly developing electronic miracles of communication, do not, one supposes, alter human nature or, if so, surely not very much. No, the changes are occurring in the means and methods of persuasion, in the techniques of conveyance of ideas and in the increase of social responsibilities between man and man and among nations.

Moreover, the life of the individual is more and more affected by the political decisions of the state. Whether unfortunate or not, expanding populations, strains upon food supply, the nudging of nations against nations, all threaten the comfort, if not the very freedom of the individual.

As Professor P. F. Oliver so aptly puts it:

"Politics is the most hazardous of all professions. There is not another in which a man can hope to do so much good to his fellow creatures, neither is there any in which by a mere loss of nerve he may so easily lose his own soul, nor is there another in which a positive and strict veracity is so difficult. But danger is the inseparable companion of honor. With all the temptations and degradation that beset it, politics is still the noblest career that any man can choose." [1]

In the United States, the *person* has some say as to how the *people* function. To what degree and in what quantity and with what intelligence persons act and interact to strengthen the people, to that extent can be measured the freedom of our society.

At the beginning I spoke to you of my hope that you would become interested in the political scene, noting that I would endeavor to enlist your active interest in political involvement in some fashion and at some level of political action. Senator Howard Baker of Tennessee, in May, 1967, stated so well the

---

[1] Dr. Arthur Peterson, Section II, *Republican Victories Through Public Relations,* p. 6.

theme upon which this book rests that I should like our political discussion with each other to end with his apt comment:

"Don't underestimate the importance of your activity and the activity of [party] workers throughout this nation. They are a part of the vitals of self-government. . . . This is the only way that you can make your viewpoint felt and *this is the only way you can speak in unison for the Government that was created for us.* You may be assured that if you don't govern yourself your neighbor will do it for you."

As Benjamin Franklin said: "We have given you a republic—if you can keep it."

Appendix A

Constitution and By-Laws
of the

_____ Young _____*Club

Adopted at_____19

Revised at_____19

CONSTITUTION

Article I—Name

The name of this organization shall be _____

Article II—Purpose

The club is founded to advance the interest of Young _____
_____** and the active participation of young people
in politics.

Article III—Membership

Any young man or woman believing in the principles of the
_____* party and intending generally to support
its candidates is eligible for membership.

Article IV—Officers

The officers of this club shall be a president, a vice president,
a secretary, a treasurer, and auditor [depending upon the size of
the club] and three directors.

Article V—Executive Board

The Executive Board is made up of the above-mentioned
officers together with the chairman of standing committees.

---

* (Insert Republican, Democratic, Socialist, etc.)
** (Insert Republicanism, Democracy, Socialism, etc.)

184

BY-LAWS

Article I—Duties of Officers

Section 1. The president shall preside at all meetings of the club and of the Executive Board and shall have general oversight of the work of the organization.

Section 2. In the absence of the president, the duties of that office shall be performed by the vice president.

Section 3. The secretary shall keep a record of all meetings and give a written report of the same.

Section 4. The treasurer shall receive all funds and shall pay all the bills when duly approved. Each bill must be certified by the person who contracted it and countersigned by the secretary upon instruction from the Executive Board. The treasurer shall keep an account of all monies received by (him or her) and report in full at the annual meeting or at the request of the president.

Section 5. The auditor shall audit all bills and accounts before the annual meeting and report in writing at such time.

Section 6. Three directors shall be elected by the members the first year for one-, two-, and three-year terms, respectively. After the first year each director shall be elected for a three-year term.

Section 7. The Executive Board shall have authority to transact any necessary business between meetings, to make recommendations concerning all policies, to serve as adviser of the president and to fill such vacancies as may occur between elections.

Article II—Meetings

Section 1. The regular meetings shall be held on the _____ _____ of each month.

SECTION 2. The Annual Meeting of the club shall be held during _____ of each year.

SECTION 3. Special meetings shall be at the call of the president, at the call of a majority of the Executive Board, or by written petition of twenty members in good standing.

SECTION 4. Meetings of the Executive Board shall be held during the week previous to all regular meetings and also at the call of the president or upon the written request of five members of the Executive Board.

ARTICLE III—NOMINATIONS

SECTION 1. A Nominating Committee of not less than three members shall be elected by the Executive Board at a meeting held at least thirty days prior to the Annual Meeting. The membership of this committee shall be announced at a club meeting held prior to the Annual Meeting.

SECTION 2. This committee shall report in writing to the Annual Meeting the name of at least one nominee for each office. Nominations may also be made from the floor.

ARTICLE IV—MEMBERSHIP

[For a club which requires payment of dues as basis for membership]

SECTION 1. Membership dues shall be _____ each year, payable at the beginning of the fiscal year. The official and fiscal year shall begin at the time of the Annual Meeting.

ARTICLE V—QUORUM

SECTION 1. A quorum of this club shall be _____ members.

SECTION 2. A quorum of the Executive Board shall be five.

186

Article VI—Amendments

Section 1. The constitution or by-laws may be amended by a majority vote of those members of the club present at any meeting, regularly called, provided that the proposed amendment shall have been presented in writing and approved by the Executive Board and that a notice of such vote for revision has been sent by mail to each member or been published in the local newspapers at least twenty days prior to each meeting.

Article VII—Parliamentary Authority

Roberts' Rules of Order shall be the parliamentary guide for matters not covered in this constitution and by-laws.